My Sister's Eyes:

A Family Chronicle of Rescue and Loss During World War II

D1556174

Joan Arnay Halperin

MY SISTER'S EYES

16 II 2019

Dear Cookie,

Here is my story. I can't wait
to hear yours.

Warm Wishes

Joan Amay Halperin

®2017 copyright Joan Arnay Halperin
Cover and Interior Design: Rosanne Guararra
Published with the cooperation of the Sousa Mendes Foundation, PO Box 4065, Huntington, NY 11743
Printed by Braintree Printing, Inc., 230 Wood Road, Braintree, MA 02184

Library of Congress Cataloguing-in-Publication Data
Halperin, Joan Arnay.

My Sister's Eyes: A Family Chronicle of Rescue and Loss During World War II / by Joan Arnay Halperin

ISBN 978-0-692-84489-2

1. Holocaust, Jewish (1939-1945) – Nonfiction. 2. Jews – Persecutions - Poland. 3. Jews – Persecutions - Belgium. 4. Jews – Persecutions-France. 5. L'Exode 1940, France. 6. Aristides de Sousa Mendes – Diplomat Rescuers. 7. Righteous Gentiles in the Holocaust. 8. World War II, 1939-1945 – Jews - Rescue. 9. Jews - World War II – Portugal. 10. Holocaust, Jewish (1939-1945) – Memoir. 11. Jews - Jamaica, BWI – Camp Gibraltar. 12. Holocaust, Jewish (1939-1945) – Poland – Warsaw Ghetto – Correspondence. 13. Jewish – Family – Historical Narrative - Young Adult.

     I. Halperin, Joan Arnay. II. Title.

info@mysisterseyes.com
www.mysisterseyes.com

To the memory of Hala and Ignas
My dear parents, I created this book for you.

To the memory of Aristides de Sousa Mendes
who acted to save my family and thousands of others.

To Angelina, Sousa Mendes' wife,
who agreed that he should follow his conscience.

To Senhor Alberto Malafaia,
one example of the kindness of the Portuguese people.

Contents

Acknowledgments

I would like to express my gratitude to Dr. Mordecai Paldiel, Dr. Marcia Sachs Littell and Dr. Michael Berenbaum, members of the Sousa Mendes Foundation Advisory Council, who encouraged me with early praise for this book. Thank you to Barbara Wind, Director of the Holocaust Council at the Jewish Federation of Greater Metrowest, for her generous advice; and to Stephen Feuer of Gihon River Press, who came out of retirement to shepherd this project, guiding me at every step of the publishing and marketing process.

On a personal level, I am thankful for the encouragement I received from my children, Guy, Coren and Roney; and from my brother, Richard Arnay, my sister-in-law, Linda; and my niece and nephew, Gabrielle and Robert.

I would like to thank Edith Sobel, Michelle Cameron, Allison Colucci, Jennifer Walkup and Lisa Romeo for their professional input in crafting this story. I'm grateful, too, for the insightful critiques of my writing partners, Ivana Gaillard, Martha Megill, Lynda Sauer and Stacie Leone Bornstein, the women whom I have dubbed the North Bergen Independent Writers' Club. You have made my new life in New Jersey a true joy.

I cannot give thanks enough to Rosanne Guararra, my talented graphic designer. Because of her appreciation of the selfless acts of Sousa Mendes, she made this project her own, skillfully bringing my mother's photos and documents to life; and to graphic designer Fiona Cashell, who assisted in the final stages of editorial layout.

I wish to thank Olivia Mattis, President of the Sousa Mendes Foundation, who after reading my first drafts and reviewing the preliminary pdf's, commented, "I can't wait to hold this book in my hands."

And most of all, I wish to give the recognition he deserves to Itzhak Halperin, my husband of forty-three years, whose moral support means everything to me.

Thank you all.

Forward

It all began with a haphazard meeting at a swimming pool. On a warm summer day in July of 1956, a stranger approached the eleven-year-old Joan and asked to be taken to her father. Joan suddenly awoke to the realization that there was an important part of her parents' past that had been hidden from her. Joan's unceasing prodding eventually revealed a panorama of vistas, both in Europe as well as the Americas. In the pages of this book, Joan has compiled a detailed account of that history, filled with her family's photos and documents. This book is a testimony to the strength of the human spirit; of overcoming adversity and maintaining hope for better days to come.

It is also a vigilant call to others not to forget the Nazi period that occured in civilized Europe; this, by recounting individual survival stories. It is also a salute to the diplomat Aristides de Sousa Mendes, who made it possible for Joan's family to flee the danger zone, and allowed them to sustain a belief in the goodness of man, in spite of the momentary triumph of evil.

The reader will surely take comfort in the strength of the human spirit, in the face of adversity, as portrayed in this book.

Dr. Mordecai Paladiel
Former Director, Righteous Among the Nations Department
Yad Vashem, Jerusalem, Israel

American Dream

It was my dad's idea to move from our third floor walk-up apartment in Brooklyn to a house of our own in the suburbs of Long Island. Mom and I were sad to leave our friends in Sheepshead Bay, but Dad loved "the country".

So, the Arnays (that was our new name) moved to Valley Stream in 1951 at the tail end of my kindergarten year.

Though it was a small house—a Cape Cod style they called it—Dad planted every kind of tree he could fit on the patch of garden that surrounded our modest corner plot. When I got a little older, my job was to pull the weeds in the flowerbeds, while Dad trimmed the hedges.

"Fresh air is good for you," he said. I hated getting my hands dirty and the bugs made me itch.

Joan in red party hat on her 4th birthday in Brooklyn, 1949.

We made lots of friends in the new neighbourhood. The boys and girls played punch ball in the streets in the summer, and made snowmen in the winter. The moms played *Canasta* one evening a week.

Once I got the knack of reading, I became a good student; I loved school and by fifth grade, I joined all the special clubs that met before and after school. Geography was my specialty and, you might say, I was the "Map Quiz Queen" of Clearstream Avenue School. No other student could find a foreign country on the world map faster than I could. Everyone thought I was just gifted at maps; they didn't know that my dad had bought me a giant globe and placed it on our dining room table.

"It's important that you know where we come from," he said.

3

The Arnays' home on Cohill Road in Valley Stream, New York, 1955.

The Kaplan Family of Lodz

The Kaplan Family at Ciechocinek Spa, Poland, July 1939.
FROM LEFT TO RIGHT: Salo, Celia, Dawid, Marcys, Renia, Lily, Maks and Fredza.

Hala

When I asked my mother about her life in Europe she would say, "We had a great life. It was a life full of family all around," and she recalled her youth in Lodz, Poland.

"Mom, tell me about your sisters."

"Joanie, how many times can you hear the same stories? I've told you about my parents, brother and sisters so many times," Mom protested half-heartedly.

"Then tell me something new about your grandpa." Thinking about Abram Majer Kaplan, with his silvery beard and sparkling blue eyes, always brought a smile to Mom's lips.

"My grandpa was so respected in our town that he was chosen to be on the city council. Not all Jews spoke Polish, but he did. He was very generous. He even organized a charity to give orphaned girls dowries. In those days, a girl could not find a husband without bringing money or household furnishings to the marriage. That's the 'dowry'. Even feather pillows and a quilt could be considered a dowry.

"But, most of all we adored him, because he made us laugh. I remember once my Aunt Miriam, who was a modern woman, said to him, 'Papa, you would be a jewel in Lodz society, if you would only cut off that beard'. Grandpa dismissed the notion with a slight wave of the hand and stroked his beard, just to annoy her."

"What about your brother?" I asked.

Hala, age 16, dressed for the Purim holiday.

Posiedzenie Komitetu Nadzczego (Lodz City Council), circa 1925. FROM LEFT TO RIGHT: J. Kwasner, J. Doeriag, M. Schott, E. Bogdanski, M. Szenwie, A. M. Kaplan (Hala's grandfather), P. Maclinski, E. Günter, J. Badnarski. Courtesy of the City of Lodz, Poland.

"My brother Leon's nickname was Lolek. Lolek and I were still single and part of the social crowd called the 'Golden Youth.'

"Our days were filled with afternoon rendezvous at cafés on Piotrkowska Street, the Broadway of Lodz. We went to dances and the cinema in the evenings. Then there were winters skiing and summers swimming or canoeing with friends on a nearby lake."

I listened, spellbound. It all sounded so dreamy. "If you were so happy at home, why did you go to Belgium?"

"After a while all those activities became boring. I was twenty-one years old. I had everything a girl could want, you're right, but I had nothing that I felt was really important to do.

"I wanted to accomplish something. Both my grown-up sisters were married. Renia had her own dancing school and Fredza gave private piano lessons. Lily, our baby sister, was still in school.

"In 1932, my best friend, Mania—she lives in Israel now—suggested that we enroll in a one-year course at the French Language Institute in Brussels. This idea appealed to me. I thought I would tutor students in French when I came back.

"There was another reason, too. I confided to my mother, 'Mama, many Polish-Jewish bachelors now live in Belgium.' Although it was unusual for girls from religious families to study abroad by themselves, after considerable cajoling, I persuaded my parents to let me go."

Hala, Spring 1935.

CLOCKWISE STARTING BOTTOM LEFT: Renia's dance group; Hala and Renia; Lolek, Poland, 1934.

The Krakowiak Family of Warsaw

Home of Abraham and Julia Krakowiak, Passover Seder, circa 1925.
SEATED FROM LEFT TO RIGHT: Hipek, Ignas, Sarah (Grandma Tenenbaum),
Polina, Julia, Abraham, Janka, Heniek, Kazik and Jezik.

Ignas

Some times on the weekend when we sat together eating our Sabbath meal I would say, "Mom, tell me about Daddy and the boarding school," Now I wanted her to repeat his stories.

"Joanie, you are never satisfied, are you?"

"Come on," I said, "Please."

"Your daddy was a spunky child," she began.

Mom was a really good storyteller. I sat very still and listened.

"One day, when he was only ten years old, he set off to see the world."

"Right, Ignas?" Dad nodded his agreement and winked my way.

"He grabbed a loaf of bread left cooling on a baker's window sill," she continued. "He advised the angry baker, 'Charge it to my mother's account.' Then he sped away on his bicycle. He did not get very far, however, before getting cold feet and returning home.

"Your grandpa on your daddy's side, Abraham Krakowiak, was very strict, not like my father. Abraham was convinced that your father needed an extra dose of discipline and so he sent him off to a German boarding school. This exile lasted one full year. Until Grandma Julia, who missed him so, successfully pleaded with her husband to bring him back to Warsaw.

Ignas, age 25.

POLAND

Warsaw
Lodz

Abraham with his sons.
TOP ROW: **Hipek, Ignas, Kazik, Jezik.** BOTTOM ROW: **Heniek, Abraham and Juzek.**

"Daddy loved sports. Didn't you, Ignas?" She gave his shoulder an affectionate nudge.

Mom still called him Ignas even though he had changed his name to Robert when he became an American citizen.

"He joined a *Zionist* youth movement. They organized the *Maccabi* sport clubs. They even had a slogan "Be Strong and Brave." Daddy loved gymnastics and *Jiu-Jitsu* the best.

"I know," I chimed in. "He's always showing me the *Jiu-Jitsu* moves and trying to tip me off balance!"

Mom nodded, smiled, and continued. "In 1923, Daddy sailed to *Mandate Palestine* to join a group of pioneers from his group. They were working to create a Jewish State there. His first work assignment as truck driver was to deliver bricks to a kibbutz near a town in the north. He hurt his knee

badly, and since he could no longer work, Daddy returned to Warsaw after only three months."

"It wasn't my fault," Daddy protested. "The bridge was too weak. It collapsed."

Mom leaned towards me and whispered, "Grandma was so relieved. She said, *W'szczęśliwy godzinę*," when she heard he was coming home. That means, 'May it be a happy event.'

Daddy didn't remain in Poland long. First, he went to France to learn how to repair watches. Then he followed in his brothers' footsteps and moved to Brussels. Belgium was a country that was developing, and welcomed Jews. Eventually, he took a job as a traveling salesman. And, that was what he was doing when we met."

Ignas, age 11, in his German boarding school uniform.

BELOW: Souvenir photo album with copper relief plaque entitled "Working the Land" made in Jerusalem, 1923.

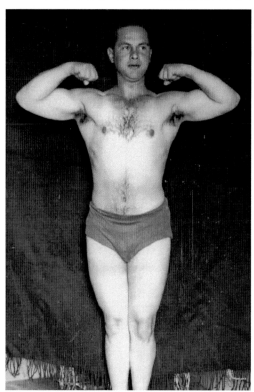

CLOCKWISE FROM BOTTOM LEFT: Ignas wrestles for Maccabi in Warsaw. TOP: Fun with a gramophone. LEFT TO RIGHT: Kazik, Jezik, Hipek, and Ignas, 1932. BOTTOM RIGHT: Jezik, Hipek, a friend, Ignas, and Kazik, 1932.

The Courtship

"Now, tell me again how you met," I coaxed.

"Meeting Daddy turned out to be my greatest fortune. I told you that before. I would have ended up like the rest of my family. May God bless their souls."

Ignas and his 1929 Opel, Brussels, Belgium.

Mom didn't speak about the sad parts, about how her family "ended up". It was as if there was a wall in her heart labeled *Before the War* and *After the War*.

"We met in April of 1935. Daddy had returned to his home in Warsaw for the Passover holiday with one goal in mind. He told his mother that he had arranged a blind date with a young woman who lived in Lodz. Grandma Julia was hopeful because Daddy was already thirty-three years old, and once again, she whispered under her breath, "*W'szczęśliwy godzinę.*'"

"She always said that, didn't she?"

"Yes, she did. Anyway, I was excited for my blind date, too. On the day of our rendezvous the eligible bachelor, your dad, rolled up in his shiny black car."

I tried to picture Lodz, Poland in 1935, where horse-drawn carriages still filled the streets.

"We all stared at this elegant man who stepped out onto the curb. He paused to look up at the façade of our apartment building, then tipped the rim of his bowler hat and strode through the entrance arch. My

Hayride, Poland, Summer 1935.
Hala, Lily, Salo and Renia on
board with friends.
STANDING: **Ignas and Lolek.**

three sisters, who just 'happened' to be there with me, said, 'Oh, he's handsome.'"

"What happened next?" I pressed her on. I loved the first date story.

"There was a firm rap at the door. I answered. I felt my heart thumping. Daddy paused in the doorway and then announced himself. 'I am Ignas Krakowiak.'

"I recognized his last name immediately, and told him that I'd met two brothers named Krakowiak at a *Zionist* Ball in Brussels when I was studying there. 'That must have been Hipek and Jesik, my younger brothers,' he exclaimed. We all laughed.

"After courteous introductions, your father and I left to join our friends waiting in the car below. This was the first time that instead of walking, I drove in a car to the sidewalk café at the Grand Hotel on Piotrkowska Street."

"What happened next?"

"You already know."

"I know. Just tell me again," I urged.

"We kept constant company for the next three weeks. We traveled the country roads in hay-filled wagons and canoed on cool lakes during the days. Then we took in moving picture shows in the evenings.

"After just three weeks, your dad professed, 'I love you'. We were standing in front of my building at the end of a wonderful evening. Then he declared: 'I want to marry you and I will not return to Warsaw until you say yes.'"

At this point, my dad nodded and caressed mom's hand. Then he got up to change his clothes to go work in the garden.

"I was torn about leaving my family. We were so close. But, it did not take me long to accept." Mom concluded.

The Wedding

The date for the wedding was set for August 11. Hala's mom, Celia, had invitations printed to announce the event. She was delighted that Hala had found a man from such a well-respected family and so handsome as well.

Family and friends packed the rooms of the spacious apartment. A warm August breeze crept in through the tall front windows and mixed with the scent of the ladies' perfume and the *Brilliantine* that slicked the men's dark hair.

Celia and Julia walked with Hala, arm-in-arm. Since Ignas's father had died two years before, Hala's father, Dawid, and Grandpa Abram Majer escorted Ignas to the traditional wedding canopy, a white prayer shawl decorated with thin blue stripes and knotted fringe perched high upon the four wooden poles. They exchanged vows, and sipped wine from

Detail of Cherubs, Winter 1995.

a silver cup. A loud crackling noise could be heard, when Ignas stomped on a wine glass carefully wrapped in a white cloth napkin, another part of the Orthodox Jewish wedding tradition. The guests responded with a congratulatory *mazel tov* and the sound that reverberated off the embossed tin ceiling was so loud that it might have been heard all the way to Warsaw.

Until now, Grandpa Abram Majer's clear blue eyes had been focused on every detail of the ceremony. When the marriage certificate was signed and sealed, Renia's husband, Salo, pulled Grandpa aside. It was not the first time that he had implored him: "Abram, Hitler has been creating laws to curb the rights of Jewish citizens and boycotting Jewish businesses in Germany. They say he has ambitions to expand his power, conquer more land. He wrote about it in his book, *Mein Kampf*. Jews here are worried. Poland may not be far behind."

15

Hala and Ignas's wedding invitation, August 11, 1935, Lodz, Poland.

Abram brushed him off with a wave of his hand.

"Abram, don't ignore my warning. Friends of yours have started transferring money to foreign banks. They are thinking of the future. You should do the same."

The stubborn old man voiced his unwillingness. "Why should I think about going to Switzerland? Here in Lodz every stone knows me."

It was a joyous occasion even though Hala would be leaving home, a place of safety, to live permanently in Belgium, a foreign, if somewhat familiar land. As the door closed behind the last of the guests, the young people prepared to go dancing at the Grand Hotel.

When they arrived, a small orchestra was playing the latest hits. Stylish couples circled the dance floor, gliding steadily in one direction. Ignas wrapped his arm tightly around Hala's waist as he led her round and round. He was a sublime dancer and she felt secure in his arms. Even the plaster cherubs atop the decorative columns that surrounded the ballroom seemed to smile down on them, heralding their bright future.

Hala noted one immediate problem. "Ignashu, how am I going to fit my dowry and clothing into one large canvas bag and two small suitcases?"

He smiled his broad smile and winked an eye. "Halinka, don't worry. I'll take care of everything."

And he did.

The Honeymoon

With the wedding behind them, Ignas was eager to start on the long trip to their new home in Brussels. On August 16, he drafted their final packing list, hurriedly grabbing the first blank sheet he found. It turned out to be the back of a leftover wedding invitation. Ignas recorded as Hala filled the luggage with the monogrammed linens and other treasured wedding gifts—her dowry.

The next morning was a tearful one as Ignas loaded his car and the entire Kaplan family gathered around to bid farewell to Hala. They said goodbye with lengthy hugs and heartfelt vows. "I'm going to visit every summer," Celia promised her daughter. She couldn't hide her tears.

"Hala, write often. We will stay in touch," vowed Renia, who was also Hala's closest friend. Then she squeezed Hala until she couldn't breathe.

The first stop was Warsaw to bid farewell to Julia, who had gone home soon after the wedding. That farewell scene was less dramatic, since she was used to saying goodbye to her sons, three of whom lived in Brussels, one in Paris, and another who had gone off to Argentina.

The honeymoon started with a drive through Germany, retracing the exact route that Ignas had travelled many times before. They stopped to snap photos along the way, and were both so optimistic about their future together.

When the newlyweds arrived in Belgium, Ignas did not go back to his job as a travelling salesman. By the spring of 1936, he had decided to open a shoe shop on the Grand Place, an elegant square in the heart of Brussels. He was sure this small enterprise would be successful.

```
Nazi Laws on Jews
Put into Effect*


September 17, 1935
Nuremburg (Sep. 16)
Beginning today the Jews are no
longer citizens of Germany.
```

All news clippings cited courtesy of the Jewish Telegraphic Agency Archives, New York. Corresponding links for the full articles can be found in the "Resources" section, p. 83.

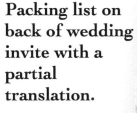

Packing list on back of wedding invite with a partial translation.

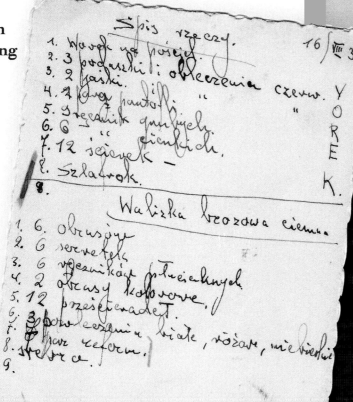

August 16, 1935

List of things:
1. bag for linens
2. 3 poduski: oblecrenia czevw (pillows)   V
3. 2 jaski I   "   "   O
4. 1 paven pantofli (slippers)   R
5. Grecznikgnubyeh   E
6. 6 " cicukich   K
7. 12 scievek
8. Szlafrok (robe)
9. Waliska brozowa ciemna (dark brown valise)

1. 6 obrusom (table cloths)
2. 6 servetek (napkins)
3. 6 veczmikage pslneieknych
4. 2 obrusy kolorovne (colored table cloths)
5. 12 przescienadel
6. 3 powleczlimia biale, rozove, miebieslive
7. 6 7 kicv reform.
8. Svelvrce
(Translation)

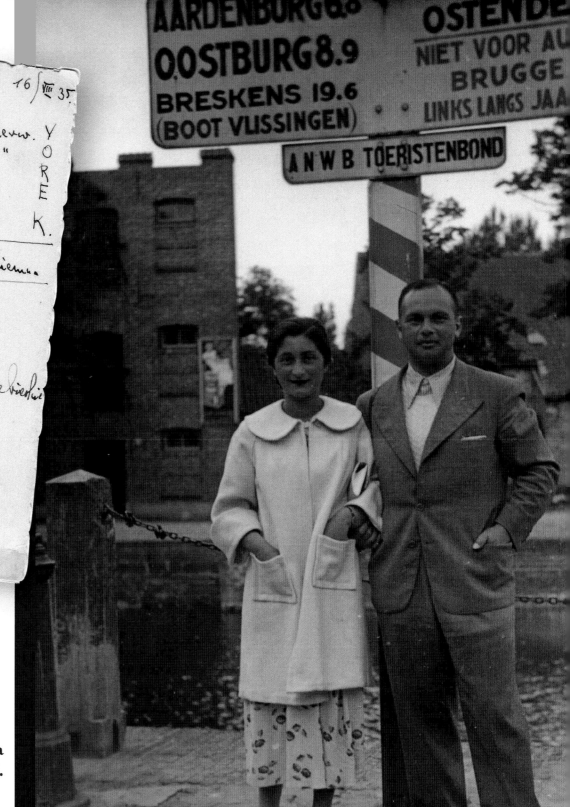

Ostende on the Belgian sea coast, September 1935.

Holiday Under Nazi Flag

In the winter of 1936-37, Ignas brought Hala to Seefeld, Austria, where life-sized ice sculptures graced the snowy streets of that fairy-tale town. Along with spectators from all over the world, the Krakowiaks visited the nearby town of Garmisch-Partenkirchen in Germany. Giant swastikas, flying boldly from every flag pole flanked the entrance to the site of the 1936 Olympic venue.

Nazi road sign partially obscured by snow reads "Jews Unwanted".

Hala and Ignas, Seefeld, Austria.

Berlin, Preparing for Olympics, Removes Last Anti-Jewish Signs

April 9, 1936
BERLIN (Apr. 8)
Last of the red-painted signs announcing that "Jews Are Our Misfortune-Whoever Buys From Jews Is A Traitor" were removed today from all public places in Berlin. Removal of the signs is part of a movement recently inaugurated to eliminate all outward manifestations of anti-Semitism in this city in preparation for the Olympic Games next Summer ... committee's preparations for the games can now proceed undisturbed.

Yvonne

By June of 1938, the couple were expecting their first child, and as was the custom of many Polish-Jewish women who were living abroad, Hala returned to Lodz several weeks before the birth.

Perhaps the women put more trust in their family's doctors. Without a doubt, they yearned for the comforts of home. Ignas arrived for Yvonne's birth. The new family spent the summer in a cottage in the country near Lodz, where the Kaplan family had a chance to welcome and adore their newest member.

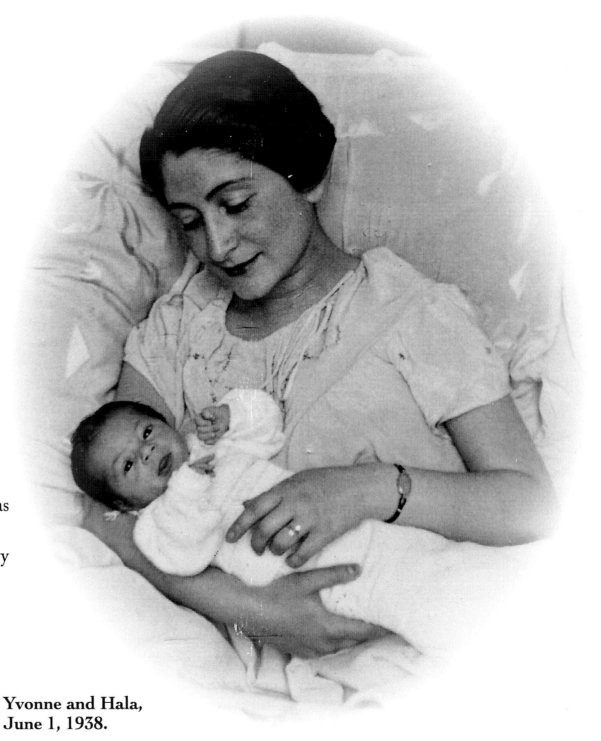

Yvonne and Hala, June 1, 1938.

Ignas and Yvonne.

40 Private Refugee Bodies Form United Front at Evian

July 8, 1938
EVIAN-LES-BAINS, France (Jul. 7)
Delegations of 40 private
organizations interested in
refugees created a united front
here today, as a deputation of
prominent Austrian Jews arrived
to present to the 32-nation
conference the plea of the
Austrian Jews for facilitation
of emigration.

1937-39

Life in Belgium

Ignas, Celia, Hala, Oskar and Janka, 1936.

Brussels

Hala and Celia Kaplan, 1936.

Hala and Yvonne, 1938-39.

Hala, Julia and Yvonne, 1939.

Hala and Yvonne, 1939.

Le Zoute

Ignas and Yvonne, 1939.

Hala, Ignas and Yvonne on the beach, 1939.

POLAND

Fears of War

CIECHOCINEK 1938 r.

ABOVE: Lolek and friend at Ciechocinek Spa, 1938. RIGHT: Renia's postcard, March 2, 1940.

In the early Spring of 1938, Germany invaded the north western part of Czechoslovakia. Polish citizens became very worried. Lolek along with other loyal Polish males his age enlisted in the Polish Army. He joined an infantry unit of the 26th Battalion that was stationed in Skierniewice, a town located between Lodz and Warsaw. Hala's mother and sister Fredza visited Lolek. Renia who kept Hala up to date with family news reported, "He misses home."

The last known photograph of the Kaplan Family, July 1939.

BELOW: Fredza, Maks and Lily, July 1939. Fredza and Maks would escape the Warsaw Ghetto and become *partisans*.

Many Poles gave in to the looming fear of an invasion by Germany, while others, the Kaplan family among them, insisted on going ahead with their lives as usual. Hala's family sent her photos from their annual holiday at Ciechocinek Spa, where they enjoyed the manicured gardens and fresh air that suspense-filled summer.

Germany Invades Poland

On September 1, 1939 Germany invaded Poland, and the Nazi army defeated the Polish Army in a matter of a few days. Lolek's unit fought in the largest battle in the campaign, which took place at the Bzura River, west of Warsaw.

ABOVE: "Response" postcard with Belgian postage sent from Lolek in Otwock, Poland under Nazi rule, April 29, 1940. RIGHT: Lolek after his release from Stalag II A prison camp, April 1940.

The Polish soldiers who survived the battle were taken prisoner and sent to Stalag II A in Neubrandenburg, Germany. Renia sent Hala a postcard from Lodsch, Deutschland, informing her that Lolek could receive packages (see p. 25).

(see p. 25)

ABOVE AND BELOW: Belgian Red Cross Receipt (front and back) for the package; stamped *Gepruft* (Checked), February 28, 1940.

Jewish Congress Urges World Action Against Treatment of Jews in Poland

December 7, 1939
PARIS (Dec. 6)
"The Jews of the world reject with revulsion and indignation the inadmissible pretext of the Reich Government that it will solve the Jewish problem in this way," … "We have no doubt that the civilized world will also reject these decisions of the present German Government for … the removal of all Jews in the Greater Reich by April 1, 1940.

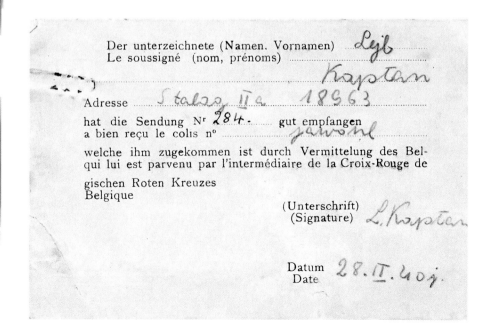

Waiting on the Coast

The sky was overcast and a relentless wind chilled the sea air. Hala and Ignas, along with their toddler, Yvonne, and Julia, had rented their holiday apartment in the tiny seaside town of La Panne earlier than usual that year. They were apprehensive about the future, and wanted to be as far away as possible from the eastern Belgian border with Germany, the aggressor.

As Hala sat on a bench outside the post office, she examined the dates on the postcard in her hand. The bold black lines crossed out their last address in Brussels. Knots formed in her stomach. This card had followed her to this temporary destination, a sandy beach at the edge of the English Channel.

Hala knew that Renia was now living in Lodsch under Hitler's *General Gouvernament*, but the return address was not Renia's. Renia's family had been forced to leave the comfort of their own apartment and squeeze in with two other families. Hala's parents were no longer in their hometown, Lodz, but were hiding in Otwock, a suburb of Warsaw.

Ignas and Yvonne, La Panne, Belgium, April 1940.

Back in August 1939, just prior to the Nazi invasion of Poland, Julia had received a warning from her youngest son Jesik: "Mamusia, Don't come back! The situation here in Warsaw is very tense." Newspapers told of the tragedy of the German occupation of Czechoslovakia, and no one knew what would happen next. Julia, who went to Belgium to visit her sons every summer, wisely decided to stay with Ignas and Hala in Belgium. She had been with them since then.

Now, as Julia and Hala pushed Yvonne's carriage along the promenade in La Panne, they met a steady stream of friends from Brussels, who like them, were flocking to the coastal towns in anticipation of …they knew not what. Everyone was frightened and they all shared the same thought: *Stay as far away from the Nazi menace as possible.*

The total occupation of Poland and the incarceration of its entire Jewish population into *ghettos* had proceeded with stunning speed. There was hardly any resistance. It all happened in the time it took to tear five pages from a calendar.

Hala and Yvonne sitting on the beach in La Panne, Belgium, March 1940.

One Step Ahead of the Bombs

**Map of Europe, 1940.
Courtesy of the Sousa
Mendes Foundation.**

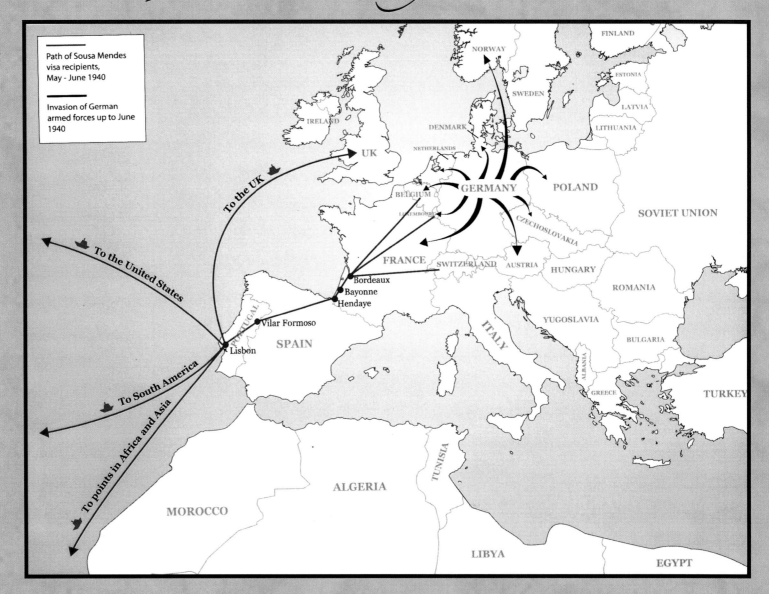

La Panne, Belgium, Friday May 10, 1940

Thousands of desperate people were now amassed on the Belgian coast. They believed that they would be protected, and that the enemy would never penetrate the *Maginot Line*. But, they were worried.

And then their turn came. Ignas and Hala were awoken before dawn by roaring motors. Incredulous, they watched from their balcony as billowing German parachutes streamed down like giant white teardrops. Stunned by the force of the *blitzkrieg*, all they could do as they waited for Ignas's brother Hipek and his wife Zosia to join them from Brussels, was to listen to news reports.

As the day unfolded, the blare of BBC broadcasts and silence would alternate, as a sense of alarm electrified the huddled groups that congregated along the beachfront in front of their apartment. First Holland and now Belgium. The dreaded invasion had begun.

Ignas became impatient and went down to the street to wait for Hipek. It was unusually hot for May. This Friday evening felt like it did in mid-summer, when holidaymakers would arrive in La Panne for a weekend break; except now there were no smiles, no hugs and no kisses on both cheeks. Instead, there were families large and small with suitcases large and small.

Hala, Julia, Ignas and Yvonne in La Panne, early Spring 1940.

Paris
FRANCE

People on carts and children in their mothers' and fathers' arms, throngs of people intent on escaping the destruction of Brussels, all passing in front of him.

Finally, Ignas saw his brother, and shouted and waved them over. Hipek grabbed Zosia's arm, guiding her steadily towards his brother. Hala and Julia greeted them at the door. "*Dgenki Bogu*, thank God, you are here," said Julia. Hipek swept Yvonne up in his weary arms and Zosia, exhausted from the journey, sunk down on to the sofa. After a hot meal they began to recount the ordeal of their journey from Brussels.

Zosia described the scene. Just like in La Panne, a terrifying whizzing had woken them before dawn. When they rushed to the balcony and threw open the windows, they heard a neighbor shout: "Les Boches! Les Boches sont la, the Germans are here!"

Zosia had stuffed her wedding silver and embroidered linens into two suitcases, until she couldn't fit in any more. "These are the things I couldn't leave behind," she explained.

Hipek had filled his pockets with the little cash that he had in his desk drawer and packed a small bag. He reasoned that he would go back to Brussels on Monday and

get more money and Zosia's jewelry from the bank.

When Ignas heard this, the blood rose to his cheeks. All this talk about indispensable things made him nervous. He jumped out of his seat and interrupted.

"No! We must head south tomorrow morning. There is no going back to Brussels right now." They all nodded with sadness in their eyes.

Zosia told Hala and Julia how the lines at the station had wrapped in and out around the platform and onto the street and when train after train departed and the crowds did not diminish, nerves began to fray. She and Hipek sat on their suitcases and waited, slowly inching up to the ticket booth. When their turn came, the only places left were in the luggage compartment. They grabbed those tickets.

The train stopped at every station and after a while people without tickets just shoved their way on board. The conductors gave up trying to follow the rules and allowed passengers to sit one on top of the other, even occupying the platforms between cars. People with tickets complained but the conductors looked at the frightened people and said, "This is war!"

Ignas told them that they would be having a very early start. Hala made Hipek and Zosia comfortable on the

Ignas and Hala with Julia seated inside of the Mercedes that they drove to safety.

living room sofas and the others went to their beds.

As the sun rose the next day, they loaded Ignas's sturdy car, purchased from his oldest brother, Heniek, who had left Belgium with his family to "visit" the New York World's Fair, three months earlier. Heniek had read *Mien Kampf* (My Struggle) and believed Hitler meant what he wrote. He wanted to erase the Jews from the earth.

Hala gathered their bedding and a few pieces of clothing. Ignas shouted to Hipek to help him tie the mattresses to the roof. The men strapped two valises on top of the mattress, secured two others to the back bumper and one to the front. All the weight caused the car's tires to flatten under the load.

Ignas ordered Hipek and Zosia to empty their suitcases, to take out half of what they had packed, to choose the most important things and leave the rest. He assured them that they would be back in a few weeks when it was all over. Zosia was reluctant, and she pleaded. This was her dowry, after all, everything that her parents had given on her wedding day. Hala and Julia traded glances. Hipek, bolstered by Ignas's resolve, took a stand and told Zosia to do as Ignas said.

Refugees heading south during "The Exodus", France, 1940.

The cars wheels regained their form and the family started on their way, destination unknown. They wanted to buy enough food for a few days on the road, but stopping at the grocery, they found that all the shelves had been stripped. They grabbed a few cans of sardines and some other tin goods that remained. Ignas tried to reassure them that they would find food along the way, but now he too was worried.

Cars crawled along the crowded roads, traveling only as fast as the people who walked alongside them. German war planes soared and parachutists peppered the sky. The booms seemed never ending. At a moment's notice, all travelers were poised to jump into the ravines that lined the dirt roads. Refugees moved south and retreating soldiers came north. They all covered only a few kilometers a day.

When they arrived at the town of Poperinge, the family found a bottleneck at the bridge over the Yser Canal. They saw more cars, bicycles, and people on foot pushing baby carriages, carts loaded with family treasures, or with children or an infirm mother or father. The lines stretched like rows of ants with an inner sense of purpose telling them exactly what to do and where to go—head south.

The Krakowiaks's turn arrived and they crossed the bridge, then headed west toward the border with France and the port town of Dunkirk. They had heard from other travelers that they could get fuel there to replenish their dwindling supply. But after a few kilometers there was that unmistakable buzzing again, coming from the direction of bridge they had just passed. The German bombers, affixed with whirring sirens to amplify the terror of their attack, dove and decimated everything beneath them.

At this point, Hipek, who had been mostly silent, numb with fear, got out of the slow moving car, threw himself to the ground and declared that he would not go on any further. He was going back.

Ignas slammed on the brakes, brought the car to a halt and shouted, "You can go back to certain death, but they are not going to get me!" Yvonne began to cry.

Julia commanded Hipek to get back in the car. Hipek obeyed his mother's orders and the family continued as one unit. If the conversation in the car had been at a minimum before, now there was stone silence.

When they reached the border with France, there were no guards on duty, no one to challenge the fact that the Krakowiaks' did not have the proper travel documents. They slipped into France without being noticed, and continued west toward Dunkirk. When they did come across a petrol station, the pumps were usually broken and the reserves of fuel were dry. Thousands of cars were on the roads by now.

The Heinkel He 111, a German bomber.

When night fell, they repeated the same routine: stop the car by the side of the road, take the mattresses off the roof, cover themselves with blankets and fall asleep under the stars. At dawn they would get back on the road. They inched past lines of exhausted British soldiers, heads hung low from fatigue and the shame of retreat.

One morning, after a night of rain, a British troop transporter making its way north abruptly shifted a gear, lunged forward and slid across the muddy road. The British vehicle's front wheel ticked the Krakowiaks' back fender, spinning their Mercedes into a ditch.

Some soldiers jumped off their vehicle and dragged the heavy car back onto the road. The captain gave the refugees two Jerry cans full of petrol from their supply.

Ignas strapped the lifesaving liquid on to the back fender, and thanked the captain repeatedly. The captain reassured Ignas that they didn't need it. They were going home.

The Krakowiaks' mission in Dunkirk accomplished, they drove southwest. Zosia glanced back through the rear window and saw the flames and smoke from the excess petrol burning. The British soldiers did not want the German enemy to use it when they took over Northern France. With the Allies suffering defeat, the Krakowiak family was more worried than ever.

Ignas followed the most obscure country roads he could find as long as they led southwest. Sometimes they found an abandoned barn, but most nights they slept in the fields.

Now that they were in France they covered the car with hay to make it look like a haystack. They had been warned by others that the French police were confiscating vehicles.

Having run out of their original supply of food weeks before, the family was always hungry. It was especially hard to find food for Yvonne who was almost two years old and needed milk. They now relied on the generosity of the French people who did their best to share their produce with the throngs of exiles clogging their roads.

One day they stopped in a French village. An elderly woman who had heard soft cries coming from the Krakowiaks' car, came over to them and asked if she could be of assistance.

Hala told the lady that her child was hungry. The kind woman took pity on them and invited the whole family to her chateau for the night. That night they ate a hot meal and slept in clean beds.

Yvonne was becoming thinner and weaker. After weeks on the road, she hardly had the energy to cry. She just lay in her mother's or her grandmother's arms, her eyes growing larger and sadder each day. When they arrived to the wine growing region of Bordeaux, they decided to stay for more than one night. Ignas found work helping a farmer in a vineyard in exchange for bread, wine, eggs, cheese, and milk for the baby.

Back on the road in mid-June, the Krakowiaks reached the outskirts of the city of Bordeaux. Here the situation was critical. Traffic was bottlenecked, stopped, stuck, masses of cars everywhere. Many vehicles of all description sat abandoned on the side of the road for lack of fuel.

Rumors were flying, information whispered from one desperate mouth to the next, "Go to the Portuguese Consulate!"

The only way out of France and away from the invading German army was with a visa to enter Portugal. Ignas parked their car under some trees, took the family's passports and entered the city on foot. He was determined to find the Portuguese Consulate and get visas to safety.

CIRCULAR 14

ALL VISA APPLICANTS NEED PRIOR APPROVAL FROM LISBON

EXCLUDED:

*FOREIGNERS OF INDEFINITE OR CONTESTED NATIONALITY;

*THE STATELESS; RUSSIANS; HOLDERS OF NANSEN PASSPORTS, OR

*JEWS EXPELLED FROM THEIR COUNTRIES AND ALSO

*ALL THOSE ALLEGING THAT THEY WILL BE EMBARKING FROM A PORTUGUESE

PORT, BUT HAVE NO CONSULAR VISA IN THEIR PASSPORTS FOR THEIR COUNTRY

OF DESTINATION, OR AIR OR SEA TICKETS, OR AN EMBARKATION GUARANTEE

FROM THE RESPECTIVE COMPANIES

On November 11, 1939 António Salazar, the President of Portugal, issued Circular 14, a formal decree ordering Portuguese diplomats throughout Europe to deny visas to "undesirables."

FRANCE
Paris
Bordeaux

The

When masses of people fled south, a bottle neck formed in Bordeaux. The scene was like an etching drawn in dark browns, grays, and blacks, everyone and everything immobile.

What was the problem? Why were there so many dirty, hungry, exhausted people packing the streets that led to the Portuguese consulate? Why were the doors to the Portuguese consulate shut tight? The refugees could do nothing but stand in line and wait.

Angel of Bordeaux

Aristides de Sousa Mendes, the Portuguese Consul General stood at a second floor window watching the crowds grow. As the days passed and the situation outside his consulate deteriorated, Sousa Mendes' dilemma became more and more acute.

Should he, a career diplomat, follow the inhumane edict of one man, to not issue visas, or summon the moral courage to stand up against that man, disobey orders, and help his fellow humans in their time of need?

While walking through the congested streets of Bordeaux, Sousa Mendes met a Polish rabbi, Rabbi Chaim Kruger. Kruger told the consul that he and his family had been living in Belgium, when the bombs had begun to fall. Now they were refugees, stranded in Bordeaux along with thousands of others urgently seeking a way out.

Sousa Mendes, a devout Catholic, father of 14 children, invited the Kruger family to his home.

The two men spoke at length. The rabbi told his host about his people trapped in Poland who were being rounded up and forced to live in enclosed districts under intolerable conditions.

Sousa Mendes was aware of the dire state of Jews under the Nazi occupation. His twin brother, César, had been the Portuguese Ambassador to Warsaw when the Nazis invaded.

Sousa Mendes family, 1929.

that had endured the perilous exodus and were waiting outside the consulate doors.

Sousa Mendes was stunned by the rabbi's refusal. He went to the windows that faced the crowded street and peered down at the throngs pushed up against the barricades. He cringed at the sight of the helmeted soldiers, bayonets in hand, guarding the entrance. Stepping back, the consul retreated to his bedroom.

Sousa Mendes explained that President António Salazar was pro-Hitler and hoped that by refusing safe haven to refugees, Portugal would remain neutral. But, after many days spent in conversation with Rabbi Kruger, Sousa Mendes sent a formal request to the Ministry of Foreign Affairs in Lisbon requesting visas for the Kruger family. On June 13th the dreaded refusal arrived.

It was then that Sousa Mendes made a decision. He told the rabbi that he would disobey the restrictions and issue visas allowing the Rabbi and his family to enter Portugal. But Rabbi Kruger declined the offer. His conscience would not allow him to accept the consul's act of compassion unless Sousa Mendes also issued visas to all those unfortunate souls

Once alone, Sousa Mendes, lay down and closed his eyes. He prayed for a moment of peaceful reflection, but was not able to subdue the images swirling before him. He tossed to and fro, but sleep would not come. Hours passed. He did not leave his bedroom. His wife, Angelina, heard his murmurings as she pressed her ear to the bedroom door. She pleaded with him to allow her to enter, and they prayed together.

Finally, after three days and nights, Sousa Mendes emerged, refreshed and invigorated. His previously graying hair was now completely white, shocking Angelina and the children.

During his self-imposed isolation, Sousa Mendes had had a revelation. He declared, "I would rather stand with God against man than with man against God." He decided to defy Salazer. He would give visas to all who asked.

Angelina agreed that he must follow his conscience and reject the inhumane proscriptions set down by the dictator, Salazar. They both knew there would be consequences, and were willing to accept them.

The couple's son-in-law protested, insisting that Sousa Mendes was forbidden by Circular 14 to issue visas without prior permission from Lisbon. He warned that Salazar would never pardon him if he disobeyed orders and that the consequences could be severe, not just for himself, but for all the family. But Sousa Mendes was decided.

"These are my people," he proclaimed, referring to the refugees on his door step. He would use his pen as a sword and the Portuguese consular seal as a shield to protect them. Propelled by a sense of confidence in what he must do next, he walked to the hallway, swung open the tall consulate doors that lead to the stairwell where anxious refuges now waited.

"Don't worry, people. Be patient. I will give visas to all who ask."

Rabbi Kruger and Sousa Mendes, June 1940.

Now that the decision had been made, action had to be swift. The Nazis had overrun Paris on the 14th of June and were storming south towards Bordeaux. Sousa Mendes and his sons, Pedro Nuno and José António, along with the Secretary of the consulate and Rabbi Kruger, set up an assembly line to accomplish the task. Rabbi Kruger collected the refugees' passports, Pedro Nuno applied the consular seal, while the consul signed the documents. Finally, visa recipients' names were registered in the consulate's official ledger.

Later, with time running short, Pedro Nuno and others signed Sousa Mendes' name on the documents as well, and they abandoned recording the names in favor of speed.

When Ignas arrived at the consulate, the great wooden doors were not yet opened for business that morning, but already another disorderly mass was clamoring out front. Drawing on some innate strength, he assumed an authoritative demeanor and shouted at the crowd as if he had been officially appointed to aid in the operation. *If you expect to get into the consulate, you need to form a line,* he told them.

He had now maneuvered to the head of that line, and so he was one of the first to walk in. Ignas got all of his family's documents signed and stamped.

LEFT: **Passport bearing the stamp of the Consulate of Portugal signed by Aristides de Sousa Mendes on June 15, 1940. Courtesy of the Sousa Mendes Foundation.**

Contented, Ignas strode back to his family, got into the car and proceeded further south to Bayonne.

In Bayonne, France, the Krakowiaks used their Portuguese visas to get Spanish transit visas and permissions to exit France. They crossed the French-Spanish border at Hendaye, France and entered Spain just over the bridge at the equally tiny town of Irún. They were safe.

In the space of twelve days, Sousa Mendes' defiant stance and quick actions saved thousands of lives.

ABOVE: **Hitler's army marching through Paris, June 14, 1940.**
RIGHT: **"Bridge of Hope" between Hendaye, France and Irún, Spain, 2016.**

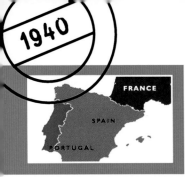

And the Sky Opened Up

Rain clouds hung over Spain, which had just emerged from a brutal civil war. The Krakowiaks drove without stopping because the Spanish transit visa allowed them only three days to make the crossing into Portugal. If they had tried to stop, hungry Spaniards would have surrounded their car begging for food, and impeded their progress.

Leaving the gloomy circumstances in Spain behind, they entered Portugal at the train-stop town of Vilar Formoso.

Jews Press Efforts to Escape from France; 760 More Reach Portugal

July 14, 1940
LISBON (Jul. 12)
Jews in France are continuing to make desperate efforts to escape...Although refugees no longer reach Portugal en masse, another 700 Jews from France entered Portugal on Wednesday and were ordered to Figueira da Foz, where the Jewish community is caring for them.

As they reached Portugal, a strange thing happened. The sun began to shine with a brightness that could only be described as heavenly. Men and women came out of their houses with trays of food in their hands asking, "Are you hungry? Are you tired? Do you want to wash? Can we offer you a bed in our home?"

Hala began to weep. These were tears of relief, the kind that come without sobs and flow in unstoppable streams.

As the Krakowiak family accepted this outpouring of generosity, Ignas approached the PIDE (Portuguese political police) to find out where they should go next. They were directed to Figueira da Foz, a small coastal town far north of the Portuguese capital, Lisbon. There, many apartments stood empty since tourism had all but stopped years before, as a result of the Spanish civil war.

In Figueira da Foz, the warmth and generosity of the Portuguese people helped the family to mend after their escape from looming disaster and to find strength for the perilous journey that still lay ahead.

Train station at Vilar Formoso, Portugal, 2016.

Refugees in Portugal

FRANCE
SPAIN
PORTUGAL

SEATED: **Friends with Zosia, holding Yvonne, Hala extreme right and Ignas behind Hala, Café Europa, Fall 1940.**

The Hebrew Immigrant Aid Society (HIAS) was there to guide the new arrivals to apartments—rooms with a toilet and bath down the hall. They were provided with utensils for cooking their meals. As they had no means to keep food fresh in their room, every morning Ignas set off for the covered stalls of the town market to buy food for that day.

The summer sun bore down on the sandy beaches of Figueira da Foz. In the cooler afternoons, the refugees gathered at sidewalk cafés to trade information about visas and learn the fate of their families left behind in the ghettos of Poland. Newspapers and the BBC radio broadcasts were the only way to get real information.

It had been two months since their escape from Belgium. They expected to stay only a short time and they were under constant pressure by the Portuguese government to leave Portugal. Refugees typically went to the countries where they already had family members to sponsor them.

Four months went by. Every once in a while, joyous friends would shout: "We got visas for Brazil! You can buy them, you know."

Six months went by, and some declared, "We got visas for the USA!" "…for Santa Domingo…Cuba…Mexico".

Their new friends kept leaving, but the Krakowiaks languished in uncertainty.

Friendships Develop

ABOVE, SECOND FROM LEFT: Yvonne standing between two young refugee friends and four older Portuguese friends. RIGHT: Alberto, Hala and Ignas. OPPOSITE PAGE: These excerpts from the Kaplan correspondence are some of the last words Hala would ever read from her family (see "Letters from the Ghetto" section, p. 75).

Senhor Alberto Malafaia was a resident of Figueira da Foz. He enjoyed meeting foreigners and soon befriended Ignas and Hala. As director of the water works and Honorary Vice-Consul of Spain in Figueira, he was able to arrange for the permissions refugees needed to travel more than 2 kilometers outside their "fixed" residences.

Thus, the auto the Krakowiaks had driven to safety became a means for diversion. Short car trips served to keep their spirits up as they waited.

ABOVE: Yvonne with *Globo Terrestre* (the Earth).
RIGHT: Ignas and Alberto Malafaia, *Portugal dos Pequenitos* (Miniature Portugal), Coimbra, Portugal, 1940.

July 10, 1941

"My Dearest,

We received that long desired package that everybody drooled over...
We are living somehow. The summer is easier, but winter will be here soon.
Kiss Yvonku and send us her picture.
They are for us the most beautiful film,

Fredza"

October 9, 1941

"Dearest,

...What is good by you? How does sweet "papcia" (a term of endearment referring to Yvonne) feel?
Renia is sitting next to me and is forcing me to write that Marcys (Renia's nine-year-old son) is a genius.
I'm sending you sweet regards and kisses,

Mother"

The Carnival Dress

ABOVE: **Maria-Luisa, daughter of Alberto Malafaia, 1936.**
Image courtesy of Maria-Luisa Malafaia.
LEFT and RIGHT: **Yvonne wearing Maria-Luisa's**
Minho **dress for** *Mardi Gras*, **February 1941.**

The Krakowiaks had been stranded in Portugal for many months. Hala received postcards and letters with news and requests for food from her family trapped in the Warsaw Ghetto.

One afternoon, the Krakowiaks and the very few refugees that were left in Figueira da Foz sat at the Café Europa, agonizing over whether they had really escaped the Nazi terror or if they would be sent back to Poland.

Senhor Malafaia approached with one hand behind his back. "What a pity there will be no parade tomorrow. The war has seen to that," he said. With the gesture of a towering magician, he pulled out the surprise he had been holding. "This is my daughter Maria-Luisa's *Minho* costume. I brought it for Yvonne to wear for Carnival. Children still have to have fun don't they?"

Hala fussed as she fastened the buttons of the dress. Yvonne, proud as a peacock, her parents in tow, began to strut all over town. "*Bom dia*, good day" she announced in her simple Portuguese, curtsying to all, her antics bringing a smile to the face of everyone she passed.

These postcards contain requests for food from Hala's family in the Warsaw Ghetto.

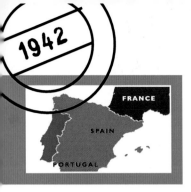

Off to Paradise

The Polish Legation office, located in Lisbon, contacted their remaining Polish-Jewish citizens, and informed them: "We have made arrangements for you to leave Portugal."

"*Dzięki Bogu*, thank heaven, we are going to be safe!" Ignas cried when he heard the news. "Where are we going?"

The representative answered, "Somewhere under the British flag."

Ignas nodded. "But, where?"

"We don't know exactly, but you will be able to work."

Ignas returned to Figueira and exclaimed, "Hala, we are leaving. We are going to be safe!"

The Krakowiak family with Senhor Malafaia in the background on train from Figueira da Foz to Lisbon, Portugal, January 23, 1942.
INSET: Portuguese yarn doll.

"Where are we going?"

"They could not tell me, but we are going to be safe!"

Then Ignas gathered the long list of documents needed for their departure, and on the 23rd of January, Ignas, Hala, Yvonne, Hipek, Zosia and Julia boarded the train for Lisbon harbor to meet their assigned ship, the S.S. Serpa Pinto.

Senhor Malafaia accompanied them part way. When it was time for him to get off the train, their goodbyes were subdued. The men shook hands and hugged, and Hala and Alberto hugged and exchanged the customary peck on both cheeks.

Their tall friend stooped down and handed Yvonne a small object wrapped in brown paper. It was a yarn-doll dressed in the brightly colored peasant style. Yvonne jumped for joy and presented the doll to her doting audience.

Then she flung her arms around Senhor Malafaia's bended neck and kissed his cheek. The conductor called *todos a bordo*, all aboard, and the Krakowiaks continued their trip in the same second-class car.

Yvonne was absorbed in introducing the passing scenery to her new friend and counting the cows as they slid by. "*Un, dois, tres, quatro, cinco, seis.* Daddy, are there cows where we are going?"

"Yes, sweetheart."

At noon, when their train pulled into Lisbon Station, they gathered their belongings and Ignas hailed a taxi. The bustling Portuguese capital was a blaze of color. Floral designs on ceramic tiles dressed the facades of even the shabbiest buildings. The chattering masses on their way home for the midday meal and *sesta* contrasted greatly with the quiet lives the Krakowiaks had lived in sleepy Figueira da Foz.

Descending the steep and narrow streets, the taxi twisted its way toward the Tagus River, where the family had secured rooms at a modest hotel. They all freshened up at the sink down the hall, and with nothing left to do, sought a meal at the restaurant next door and waited for the dark and the coming dawn.

JDC Arranges Emigration of Polish-Jewish Refugees from Lisbon to Jamaica

January 12, 1942
NEW YORK (Jan. 11)
Emigration from Portugal to the British island of Jamaica of 180 stranded Polish-Jewish refugees has been made possible through the collaboration of the Joint Distribution Committee with the British and Polish governments…. The refugees… who have been stranded in Lisbon for periods up to a year and a half, would have remained stranded if the JDC had not come to their help because all previous efforts to secure overseas visas for them had failed.

The Trans-Atlantic Voyage — January 24, 1942

After twenty months under the constant stress of reporting to the local authorities for permission to stay in Portugal, the Krakowiaks were impatient to set sail for safety even though all they had been told so far was that they would be going somewhere under the protection of the British flag. The American Joint Distribution Committee (JDC) or "The Joint" as it was commonly referred to, had arranged this evacuation for the remaining Polish-Jewish refugees who still could not find a country to let them in.

The Serpa Pinto, the ship they were assigned to had been designed for 450 passengers, but at that moment of mounting duress, with rumors of Nazis troops banging on Portugal's neutral door, a cabin on board meant for two was gratefully occupied by four or five. In addition, sleeping quarters were set up in the ship's belly, which became a crowded, malodorous muddle.

The Nazis had planted explosive mines in the North Atlantic Ocean, so the overloaded vessel, zigzagged across the dark January sea, slowing down and speeding up in order to dodge the perilous obstacles. Yet the turbulent ocean portended good fortune; the wolf packs of German U-boats would find it harder to hit their targets in the swirling waters.

On calm nights, passengers emerged from the makeshift dormitory in the enormous hull to breathe the fresh air and dream under the stars of hope. Thin, soiled mattresses were strewn from aft to bow. Vomit covered the once shiny deck, but the passengers ignored the wretched scene before them, as they anticipated a brighter future.

Several days into their journey, the JDC's representative, Mr. Jacobsen, called his group of one hundred fifty Polish-Jews on deck for a meeting. He explained that he had just been informed that they were heading to a British evacuee camp called Gibraltar Camp. He added that the exhausted refugees would live in army-style barracks surrounded by a security fence. They were forbidden to work outside the camp and must seek permission from the Commandant to leave the camp during the day. Their curfew would be 10:00 p.m. This was the first any of the refugees had heard the details of their rescue.

Members of the group became agitated. Some called out:

"What?... We were told that that we were going to live as free men... We were told we would be able to work... A fence!... Barbed wire!... A Commandant?"

Finally, one rose up and asked, *"What? Are we the enemy?"*

But now that they were on the high seas there was little they could do, but hope for the best.

Despite the enormous PORTUGAL emblazoned on its hull and the constant illumination of the ship by night, a U-boat did stop them and German soldiers boarded the ship. They checked each and every travel document before allowing the ship to continue. After this incident, most of the weary refugees resigned themselves to living in a "golden cage."

At the end of the sixteen-day passage, the verdant hills of Kingston, Jamaica appeared on the horizon as the ship slipped into port.

Polish-Jewish Refugees in Jamaica Seek Permanent Haven Elsewhere

April 7, 1942
LONDON (Apr. 6)
The 150 Polish-Jewish refugees...
today appealed to Jewish groups here
to facilitate their emigration to
permanent settlements abroad... Jamaica
authorities do not consider them
immigrants but evacuees ...not allowed
to engage in any kind of work...housed
in a special camp...not allowed to move
freely outside the camp after 10PM.
Several cases of fever have broken out
among the refugees...

Hala and Ignas in front of Hut No. 62,
their lodgings at Gibraltar Camp, Kingston,
Jamaica, British West Indies, 1942.

BACKGROUND: View of Long Mountain,
University of the West Indies, Mona, Jamaica, June 2014.

The Bicycle

Ignas used his first paycheck to buy a second-hand bicycle he could ride to work. He fashioned a wooden seat on the back for Yvonne and they became a travelling duo during the cooler afternoon hours. They were inseparable as they explored the camp.

They developed a routine. Ignas wove in and out beneath the time-worn arches of the stone aqueduct. Yvonne, who was now two weeks away from her 4th birthday clung tightly to her father's waist, perched on her seat like a tiny bird with skinny legs dangling in the air.

At the sound of her laughter, bridge players looked up from their cards, readers from their books and newspapers, while other nervous refugees diverted their attention from the BBC radio reports. Kitchen workers paused to wave and the ladies at the stone laundry troughs lifted their heads and stopped their scrubbing to watch them.

Hala always breathed a sigh of relief when they returned at the clanging of the big iron bell, the signal for dinner.

Late one afternoon in mid-May, Ignas's bike picked up speed as they glided down a small slope. The thin front wheel of the rickety English racer hit a series of ruts in the hard dirt road. The bicycle jolted and swerved. Ignas did his best to stay upright, but Yvonne's sandal became ensnared in the spindly spokes of the back wheel.

The bicycle tipped over. They hit the ground hard. Yvonne's foot was trapped under the rusty hub of the wheel. Ignas jumped to his feet, lifted the bike to reveal her twisted ankle, crushed and bleeding. He swept her up into his arms and ran towards the infirmary. On his way, he passed his brother, who sat with a group of men playing bridge.

Ignas shouted, "Hipek, go get Hala! I'm going to the infirmary."

The Infirmary

Ignas got to the infirmary, panicked and screaming for the doctor. Only the nurse was there. Calmly, she pointed to the examination table and instructed Ignas, "Put the child down." She cleansed the wound and sent for the doctor.

Hala was sitting on the screened-in veranda of hut No. 62, as she did every afternoon, anticipating Ignas's return. That day Zosia was with her. They were discussing the floral print material Zosia was using to sew a dress for a rich Dutch refugee, recently arrived from Europe.

Hipek ran up to the two women. His chest was heaving. He was sweating. He couldn't seem to find the words.

"Hipchu, what's the matter with you?" Zosia shouted.

"*Chodzmy, chodzmy! Szybko, szybko!*" Let's go! Fast! They had an accident. Yvonku is in the infirmary."

Hala jumped to her feet and scrambled up the stairway that led to the upper camp. She reached the top and there was more ground to cover. From the entrance to the infirmary, she saw the doctor tending to Yvonne, who was lying on her back, moaning.

Hala leapt forward, looked at Yvonne's shattered foot, reeled back and roared at the doctor in a voice that rose from the pit of her being.

"Do something!"

Her body shaking, she turned and glared at Ignas. "What happened? What happened to my baby?"

Ignas did everything he could to get the doctor to move Yvonne to the hospital in Kingston, but the Commandant insisted that the camp infirmary was well-equipped to handle this emergency.

As days went by and her fever raged on, Ignas begged on bended knee, "Help my baby!"

Finally, even the obstinate Commandant saw that they could not help the child and had her transferred to the hospital.

It was too late.

BACKGROUND AND INSET: University of the West Indies, Mona, Jamaica, June 2016.

"Ici Repose...Here Lies..."

POLISH GROUP

CAMP 2

COCO72

4/6/42

Deceased: No. 82   YVONNE KRAKOWIAK   4 years

Hut 62 Room 21

B. GLASSCHEIB

HICEM   Kingston, 5th June 1942

NEW YORK

re: members of group

Dear Sirs,

Yesterday we had a **rather bad** day and decidedly nothing will be spared to us, as we had the first decease amongst us: a little girl of four.

Enclosed two slips for the files (Duplo for the Joint)

Yours truly

Notifications of Yvonne's death sent to the HICEM Offices in New York. Courtesy of the YIVO Archives at the YIVO Institute for Jewish Research, New York.

It had been two days since her sweet soul slipped away. Jewish custom dictates that the dead be buried as soon as possible. But there was no rabbi. There were no prayer books. Two grave diggers placed the pine box into a hole in the dry, stony earth of the cemetery on Orange Street. A wooden sign marked the grave.

As Ignas and Hala walked out of the cemetery, a hellish enclosure of tall cement walls, blackened by the soot of time, they took slow, deliberate steps, as if a dark cloud was pressing down on them.

Hala's eyes were cast down toward the pebble path. Ignas wrapped his arm tightly around her waist like an iron brace, directing her unsteady movements. They had just buried their little treasure.

The sun shone brightly as they waited for the trolley to take them to the last stop on its route. They got on board, welcoming the shade as the trolley moved unhurriedly on the Old Hope Road. Not even the shrill squeaking of the brakes as it creaked along its way had the power to rouse Hala from her stupor.

When they passed the spot where Old Hope Road intersects with Old Hope Boulevard, Ignas was overcome by a wave of nausea.

He didn't dare look up toward the familiar blue and white Jamaica College building.

In this, the lowest moment of his existence, he could not bring himself ask the question: *Had the bicycle that brought them so much pleasure also caused his baby's death?*

The answer would have been too difficult to endure.

They got off at Papine Square. The last part of the journey had to be travelled on foot. Hala leaned on Ignas and he moved her along, step-by-step.

They reached the camp gate as the bell sounded for lunch.

Groups of people swarmed

Yvonne's grave. Orange Street Cemetery, Kingston, Jamaica, 1943.

toward the dining hall. Some were their close friends, some were acquaintances; no one dared to break the invisible circle of their grief.

As they passed the wooden barrack that housed the infirmary, Hala's knees gave way. Ignas propped her up.

Then they reached the veranda of their barrack and entered their cubicle. Intense sunlight streamed through the only window. Hala walked across the rough planked floor and pulled the shutters tight, as if this action would help her hide from the world. Ignas followed behind her.

Ignas finally spoke. "I am going to bring back some food for you."

Hala dropped to the bed and muttered, "*Zostaw mnie.*"

Ignas insisted, "You need to eat." She repeated, "Leave me alone."

He tried to comfort her. She recoiled and with her last bit of force repeated her plea, "Leave me!"

She lay her head down on the pillow and shut her eyes.

Yvonne's memorial photo.

60

CUBA
HAITI
JAMAICA
Kingston

"I Have No Children…"

Form No. 255
FOREIGN SERVICE
(Revised March 1939)

American Consulate

No. 35.

AT Kingston, Jamaica.

APPLICATION FOR IMMIGRATION VISA (QUOTA)

I, the undersigned APPLICANT FOR AN IMMIGRATION VISA, being duly sworn, state that my full and true name is
Hinda Rosa KRAKOWIAK (nee Kaplan) ; that I am 32 years of age, of the female sex and
Polish race; that I was born on the 15th day of January, 1911
at Lodz, Poland ; that since reaching the age of 14 years I have resided at the following
places, during the periods stated, to wit: Lodz, Poland 1925 - 1932; Brussels, Belgium 1932 -
1933; Lodz, Poland 1933 - 1935; Belgium 1935 - 1940; traveling through France,
Spain to Portugal 1930 to Jan.1942; Camp Gibraltar, Jamaica, Feb. 1942 to the
present time.
That I am {married}, and the name of my {husband} is Izaak Krakowiak , who was born
at Warsaw, Poland ; and resides at Camp Gibraltar, Jamaica.
That the names, dates of birth, and places of residence of my minor children are:

I have no children.

That my calling or occupation is Housewife ; that my height is 5 feet and 1 inches; my complexion
Brunette ; color of hair, Black ; color of eyes, dk.brown ; and that I bear the following marks of identification:
None ; that I am {able} to speak Polish, French, {able} to read
German, English
Polish, French ; that the names and addresses of my parents are as follows:
German,English and {able} to write the Polish,French and
German
(Name of language or dialect)
Mother, Cyrla Kaplan (nee Gross) ; address, (deceased).
Father, David Kaplan ; address, (deceased).
That neither of my parents is living, and that the name of my nearest relative in the country from which I come is Izaak
Krakowiak , whose relationship is husband and whose address is (as above).
That my port of embarkation is Kingston, Jamaica ; that I shall enter the United States at the port
of Miami, Florida ; that my final destination beyond such port is Great Neck,L.I.,N.Y. ; and
that I do have a ticket through to such destination; that my passage was paid for by my husband,Izaak Krakowiak,
whose address is (as above) ; that I intend to join {relative} brother-in-law,Henry Arnay,
whose address is 37 Brompton Rd.,Great Neck, L.I.,N.Y.
(City, state, street, and number)
That my purpose in going to the United States is to reside , and I intend to remain permanently
(Permanently or length of time)
that I have never been in prison or almshouse; that I have never been in an institution or hospital for the care and treatment
of the insane; that my {father}{mother}{have}{has} not been in an institution or hospital for the care and treatment of the insane; that I have not
applied for an immigration or passport visa at any American consulate, either formally or informally.

Finally, after another year and four months of petitioning and waiting, all the while mourning Yvonne's tragic death, it was the Krakowiaks' turn to get their US visas.

Hala filled out the immigration application. There were many questions to be answered.

She wrote: "Mother… deceased. Father… deceased," even though she was not completely sure of their fate. Then, the most painful question of all: "names, dates of birth, and places of residence of minor children."

Hala tightened her grip on the pen. She pictured the marble stone they placed above Yvonne's grave and with a heartache that was unbearable, she wrote: "I have no children."

Application for US immigration visa, August 1943.

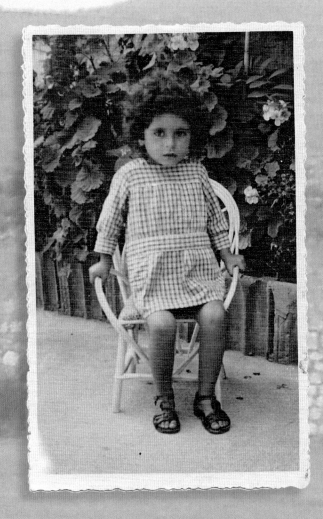

On October 2, 1943 Ignas and Hala flew from Jamaica to Miami and then took a train to New York City. Heniek and wife Janka were there at Pennsylvania Station to greet them.

The HIAS came to their aid once more, arranging and paying for Ignas and Hala's first apartment, a studio on the Upper West Side of Manhattan.

Zosia and Hipek arrived in New York one month later, and got a studio in the same neighborhood, which by now was teeming with Holocaust refugees.

Last picture taken of Yvonne, Figueira de Foz, Portugal, 1942.

BACKGROUND: 18th c. Aqueduct, University of the West Indies, Mona, Jamaica, 2014.

Brooklyn, USA

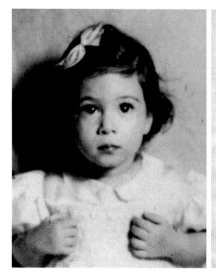

Joan's birth announcement.

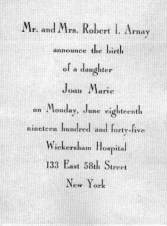

Mr. and Mrs. Robert I. Arnay

announce the birth

of a daughter

Joan Marie

on Monday, June eighteenth

nineteen hundred and forty-five

Wickersham Hospital

133 East 58th Street

New York

LEFT TO RIGHT: A friend, Fela, Ignas holding Joan, Hala, Paul and friends, Brighton Beach, New York, 1945-46.

Paul Muskat, Ignas's friend from his Boy Scout days in Warsaw, and his wife Fela, had come to the United States as "tourists" for the 1939 New York World's Fair, and had managed to stay. They lived in Sheepshead Bay, Brooklyn and suggested that my dad come and see how wonderful the ocean air could be.

The day I was born, Dad announced that we were moving to Brooklyn. He had found a place they could afford. The rent was $59 a month.

On Sundays, my dad and "Uncle" Paul, rode bicycles on the broad band of boardwalk that spans the coast from Brighton Beach to Coney Island, while my mom and "Aunt" Fela pushed my carriage and fawned over me. After the Holocaust, good friends rose to the status of aunt and uncle, since so many of the real ones were gone.

On weekdays, Mom busied herself with domestic chores. Monday was wash day. Clamping her hand over mine, she and I wheeled the dirty clothes to the laundromat around the corner from our 3rd floor walk-up apartment. Then we wheeled it back home, climbed the stairs and she hung it out to dry on the line on the fire escape outside the kitchen window.

May 5, 1945

Hala sent this postcard to her grandfather, Abram Majer, at his last known address in Lodz. She wanted to see if her family had survived the war. She knew they would go back to the houses that Abram Majer owned.

Dearest Grandpa,

The wartime turmoil has pulled us to New York. We lived through some very hard times, but I now know they were nothing in comparison to yours.

Is it possible that you are all healthy?? I would be happy if I would receive a small sign of life from you.

Write and I will send you packages - everything that I possibly can.

Sending you heartfelt kisses,

Hala

Dad made his way from stacking heavy boxes in a warehouse to representing a jewelry supply firm. Diamond merchants from Belgium, many of whom had also received visas to safety from Aristides de Sousa Mendes, were setting up businesses in New York.

In time, he started his own business: Robert I. Arnay: Balances of Precision, Scales for Weighing Diamonds and Gold, located on 47th Street in the heart of New York City. The day he sold four diamond scales to Tiffany & Co., he declared, "We are going to buy a house."

Mom, a usually compliant wife exclaimed, "A house! How can we afford a house?"

"Don't worry. I can do it," he answered and emphasized "You'll have a clothes washer of your own!"

By then, Dad's confidence had been restored, the brutal journey that had lasted one thousand two hundred and forty-one days was fading into the past.

In May of 1951, eight short years after arriving at heaven's shores broken and penniless, my father put $50 down on a home and got a mortgage with a payment of $200 a month. And that's how the Arnays of Sheepshead Bay moved to 3 Cohill Road at the corner of Buscher Avenue.

BACKGROUND:
Bear Mountain State Park Swimming Pool, New York.

1956

One afternoon in the early spring of 1956, when I was almost eleven-years-old, I came home from school and pounced on my mother, smothering her with kisses, our after-school greeting ritual.

This particular afternoon Mom said, "Joanie, you can't jump on me like that anymore."

I asked, "Why?" and Mom announced, "We are going to have a baby."

I snuggled closer. I was very pleased. All my friends had either a sister or a brother. Now I too would have someone to play with on a rainy day.

My brother, Richard, was born at the end of May. I was so excited.

July 4th

By the time the holiday weekend rolled around, the cool spring days were long gone and the weatherman predicted temperatures up around 90 degrees.

My parents decided to head north to escape the steamy Long Island heat. Mom packed a lunch for Dad—sardines and black bread, some cheese and fruit—but she and I looked forward to the frankfurters and French fries we would buy at the food stand.

Dad checked the oil and tested the tires of his shiny old Cadillac for the long stretch of the tree-lined Palisades Parkway that led to our favorite summer destination: Bear Mountain State Park.

As soon as we arrived, we looked for a good spot to spread our blanket. Mom parked Ricky's carriage under a broad old oak. Dad tied his rope hammock, a remnant of his life in Europe, to two sturdy white birch trees. I waved goodbye and went off to test the waters of the giant swimming pool.

I descended at the shallow end, step after careful step. As I pushed through the crowd, excusing myself as I went, I noticed a man with wispy hair who was wearing a dark maroon bathing suit with a white belt, just like my dad's. *He must be from Europe,* I thought.

I puttered about aimlessly, careful not to "wander too deep" and to "stay no more than one or two strokes away from the edge," as my father always warned.

After a while, I saw the same man again, now perched at the edge of the pool waving his arms like a frantic bird. I realized he was trying to catch my attention, so I waded over. The man bent down on one bony knee and said, "Take me to your father."

I recognized his accent as Polish. Though I was sure I knew every member of my parents' refugee crowd, this man was new. I hoisted myself up onto the rim, stood up and squeezed the water from my bathing suit skirt, then led him to the place where my family sat enjoying the protective shade.

Daddy was relaxing in his hammock, as I approached with the stranger at my side. But when the two men's eyes met, even I could see there was a lightning flash of recognition. Dad jumped to his feet and moved towards the man. As they hugged and kissed on both cheeks, they looked like two small bears. Neither man spoke until they pulled apart.

"Ignas, after so many years, I've finally found you," the man said to my father.

"Mommy, how does Daddy know this man?" I was puzzled.

"He is Daddy's friend from Warsaw. We also met him again, when we got to Portugal. I told you about Portugal. That man got a visa for Argentina and left Portugal much before we did. We haven't seen him since."

My head began to hurt like it did whenever my mother spoke about their escape from Europe.

The old friend turned to my mother and exclaimed in broken English, "Look at you, Hala! Two children!" My mother nodded his way, but didn't speak. She seemed uncomfortable.

"How did that man even know I was Daddy's daughter?" I continued, turning my attention back and forth between the man and my mother. "I know all your friends and I've never seen him before."

As my dad and his friend continued their conversation in Polish, the man looked back at me several times. Then tears began to flow down both men's cheeks.

"Mom, why are they crying?" I sat down next to my mom, even more confused.

"Sweetheart, there is something I haven't told you."

I leaned over, straining to hear what the two men were saying. I did understand a little Polish. Mom's words did not register at first.

"Like what?" I demanded. "I know all your stories about your family and the war."

"Not everything, sweetheart," her eyes downcast.

"Daddy just told him the sad news," she said in a voice no higher than a whisper.

"What sad news? What are you talking about?" My stomach began churning.

Mom looked directly at me, all color drained from her cheeks. Her normally vibrant eyes were dull. She took a slow, deep breath.

"You have your sister's eyes," was all she could muster.

I began to shiver. She tried to wrap her arm around my shoulder, but I pulled away and stared at her. When I found my voice, out poured more questions.

"What do you mean? What sister? What are you saying?"

Mom looked past me, her gaze seeming to traverse space and time.

"You never told me I had a sister" I persisted.

"She died while we were waiting to come to America," Mom said in a flat tone.

"Do I look like her?" I couldn't believe what she was saying. "What happened to her? Why didn't you tell me?" Now I was crying, too.

"What good would it have done for you to know?" Mom protested weakly as Ricky squirmed in her arms. Then she got up and gently laid my brother in his carriage.

Until that day, my parents had never spoken of a child they had loved before me, a girl just like me. I was shaking, but I could not stop questioning her.

"How did she die? How old was she? What happened?"

"I can't talk about it," Mom said as she moved her head slowly from side to side.

My heart hurt, I felt it shrinking. I was just getting used to having a baby brother in the house and sharing my parents' attention. Now this!

"Where did she die?" I continued.

"She died in Jamaica, when we were in the camp," she offered reluctantly. Her eyes begged for mercy as she rocked the carriage from side to side, like a storm-tossed ship on a vast winter sea.

"Now, please stop" she added more forcefully "I said I can't talk about it." At last she promised, "I will tell you more one day, but not now."

BACKGROUND: Whitestone Bridge, New York.

Skeletons

Yes, mine was the kind of family that kept secrets. They were the same skeletons that thousands of Holocaust survivors kept hidden in the depths of their New World closets. Years and years after the revelation at the Bear Mountain swimming pool, when I first found out that my parents had had a child before me, and that my eyes so resembled hers that a seeming stranger could imagine that I was the little girl he had known in Portugal 14 years earlier, my mom agreed to record her story for posterity.

It was New Year's Day in 1989, when my mother sat down with my brother and me for a video interview. She spoke readily about her family the happy days before the war. But, when I asked her once again and although it was 47 years later, she still could not bring herself to speak of Yvonne. She fumbled with the crumple tissues in her hands and asked us to turn off the camera.

In 1997 Mom gave me a slim vinyl photo album, labeled "Yvonne," and a packet of correspondence from her family when they were in the Warsaw Ghetto. I have woven Yvonne and the Kaplan family into this narrative using those photos, letters and other documents. I have interspersed the news clippings from the archives of the Jewish Telegraphic Agency, and other archival materials to ground this personal chronicle in global history.

I located three witnesses who were the children at the time using the Joint Distribution Committee's letter of commitment for support of 150 Polish-Jewish refugees who sailed from Lisbon, Portugal on the Serpa Pinto to Kingston, Jamaica with my parents. Although these witnesses were four, six, and 13 years of age in 1942, each had vivid, though somewhat differing memories of Yvonne, the bicycle accident and her untimely death.

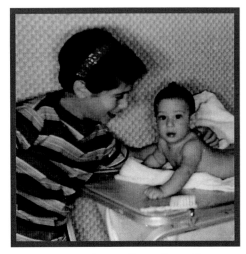

Joan watching her brother, Richard, on his *bathinette*, January 1957.

Joan and Richard, the day of her Sweet sixteen, June 1961.

STANDING: **Joan Arnay Halperin.** SEATED LEFT TO RIGHT: **Coren Halperin, Helene (Hala) Arnay holding Roney Halperin, Robert (Ignas) Arnay, Richard David Arnay.** SEATED: **Guy Halperin,** June 1981.

Further confirmation of the causes of Yvonne's death came when I went to Jamaica to visit Yvonne's grave in 2014. I obtained her death certificate, which states: Cause of Death as meningitis (which can be a complication of sepsis, blood poisoning) and tuberculosis.

This information corroborates the testimonial of the boy of four. Grandma Julia died of tuberculosis in a sanitarium in Monticello, New York in 1948. Yvonne may have contracted tuberculosis during the journey from Belgium to Portugal.

Though I never knew Yvonne, and spent most of my life not knowing very much about her, her short life and the story of my parents' dangerous quest for safety has informed my life. Yvonne's story is that of one child among many (how many? we don't know) who died during the flight to freedom. She represents an unknown number of child refugee victims who should be added to the estimated 1.5 million children known to have died in the Holocaust.

I would like the reader to know that even though their trial of 1,241 days in limbo resulted in personal tragedy, my mother frequently told me that she and my father blessed the United States, the country that gave them a new start, and the American people who welcomed them with open arms.

They did not allow either the loss of their cherished first child, nor Mom's longing for her family, to consume their days. They lived life.

SEATED LEFT TO RIGHT: **Grandma Julia, Joan, Janka, and Hala, Monticello, New York, 1947.**

Recollections of children who were with Yvonne at Gibraltar Camp in 1942*

A boy who was four:

"When she didn't come back from the infirmary, it was a tremendous shock to us. When we were older, our parents told us that Yvonne died of sepsis, a result of her injury from the bicycle accident. Even though Ignas begged on bended knees, the Commandant would not move her to a regular hospital where they might have saved her with better medical treatment. It wasn't a question of money; other refugee friends would have chipped in, but the willful Commandant refused."

A girl who was six:

"We lived in the cubicle next to Yvonne and her parents in the barracks at Gibraltar Camp. I played with her as if she were my little doll. When she did not come back from the infirmary my mother had to tell me what happened. I remember that after Yvonne died, Hala didn't go out in public for one year."

A boy who was thirteen:

"Yvonne was a lovely, intelligent and vivacious little girl. I remember babysitting for her a couple of times. Her illness came suddenly. She developed a very high fever. I think it was malaria. I believe Yvonne started in the infirmary and then was taken to the hospital in Kingston when her condition deteriorated. Her unexpected death at such a young age was a blow to all who knew her, but to Hala and Ignas it was devastating. They lived through and beyond that loss with courage and stoic fortitude."

*Testimonials given to Joan in 2014.

Sousa Mendes Legacy

Aristides de Sousa Mendes, a descendant of a noble Portuguese family, joined his country's diplomatic corps after graduation from the Faculty of Law at the University of Coimbra. He was stationed as Portuguese Consul General in Bordeaux in the Spring of 1940, when Nazi Germany attacked Belgium, the Netherlands, Luxembourg and northern France, precipitating a flood of refugees into southern France.

Acting on the dictates of his conscience and against the explicit orders of his government, he and his staff issued visas to neutral Portugal, opening an escape route out of Europe for thousands of desperate refugees.

Understanding the horrors that awaited if he did not act, Sousa Mendes gave visas to all who asked, regardless of nationality, race, religion, or political opinions. Some sources estimate the numbers as high as 30,000 persons.

For his actions, Sousa Mendes was summoned back to Portugal and punished by his government, which stripped him of his position and his livelihood. He lived the rest of his life in destitution and disgrace, taking his meals at a Jewish soup kitchen. He died a pauper in 1954.

His children fled Portugal, seeking asylum and awaiting the opportunity to clear their father's name and honor his heroism. The first recognition came from Yad Vashem, the World Holocaust Remembrance Center located in Israel in 1966, when Sousa Mendes was declared one of the "Righteous Among the Nations."

In 1986, the United States Congress issued a proclamation honoring his heroic act. In 1987, he was finally recognized by Portugal when then President Mario Soares issued a formal apology to the Sousa Mendes family. The Portuguese Parliament promoted him posthumously to the rank of Ambassador.

Despite the years of injustice and bitterness imposed on him and his family, Sousa Mendes never regretted what he had done.

He once said, "I could not have acted otherwise, and I therefore accept all that has befallen me with love."

The actions of Aristides de Sousa Mendes in the June of 1940 will stand as a moral example for individuals to act against intolerance, racism, and genocide today and forevermore.

The Sousa Mendes family receives the Yad Vashem medal. TOP ROW LEFT TO RIGHT: Sebastião Mendes, Teresinha Swec, César Mendes, Joana Mendes, Luis-Filipe Mendes, John Paul Abranches. BOTTOM ROW LEFT TO RIGHT: Aristides Mendes, Geralyn Swec, Carolyn Swec, Israeli Consulate, New York, 1967.

Righteous Among the Nations

50 Years • 1966 - 2016

KRAKOWIAK

Israel Tenebaum
b.18?? Radom
d.19?? Warsaw

Sarah Tenebaum
b.18?? Radom
d.19?? Warsaw

Abraham
b.1872 Warsaw
d.1926 Lodz

Julia
b.1876 Radom
d.1948 NYC

Heniek
b.1898 Warsaw
d.1980 NYC

Janka
(nee Goldstein)
b.1901
d.1982 NYC

Juzek
b.1900 Warsaw
d.198? NYC

Ann
b.19??
d.19?? NYC

Ignas
b.1902
d.1983 NYC

Hipek
b.1903 Warsaw
d.1957 NYC

Zosia
(nee Frumainska)
b.1910 Warsaw
d. 2012 NYC

Kazik
b.1906 Warsaw
d.19??
Buenos Aires

Jesik
b.1911 Warsaw
d.19?? Tel Aviv

Helka
b.19??
d.19??
Tel Aviv

Polina
b.1912 Warsaw
d. 2004 Tel Aviv

Adek
Skalski
b.19??
d.19??
Tel Aviv

Oskar
{Krakowiak}
Arnay
b.1928 Warsaw

Yvonne
Krakowiak
b1938 Lodz
d.1942 Jamaica

Joan
{Krakowiak}
Arnay Halperin
b.1945 NYC

Itzhak Halperin
b.1944
Petach Tikvah,
Israel

Richard David
{Krakowiak}
Arnay
b.1956 NY

Linda
(nee Dranoff)
Arnay
b.1956 NY

Guy
b. 1974

Coren
b. 1977

Roney
b. 1981

Gabrielle
b. 1982

Robert
b. 1985

KAPLAN

Abram Majer
b.1867 Pila
d.1942 Treblinka?

Dawid
b.1887 Lodz
d.1942 Treblinka?

Celia (nee Gross)
b.1887 Lodz
d.1942 Treblinka?

Renia
b.1909 Lodz
d.1942 Treblinka?

Zalo
Waldenburg
b.1909 Lodz
d.1942 Treblinka?

**Hala
b.1911 Lodz
d.1999 NYC**

Lolek (aka Lejb, Leon)
b.1912 Lodz
d.1942 Treblinka?

Fredza
b.1914 Lodz
d.1942? Unknown

Maks
Garelick
b.191? Lodz
d.1942? Unknown

Lily
b.1922 Lodz
d.1942 Treblinka?

Marcys
b.1933 Lodz
d.1942 Treblinka?

Letters from the Ghetto

No. 1 March 2, 1940
Lodsch, Deutschland to La Panne, Belgium

My Dearest Halinko,
Your card dated February 12th just arrived yesterday.
I don't know if you have received my card where I give you the gist
of the card from Lolka. He earns 13 marks a month plus room and
board. He writes that he hasn't got it bad.
Anyway you are surely going to get an extensive letter from him
soon. I gave him your address.
I would be grateful if you would send him some warm things. He
asked for warm pants and socks. We will send him the rest. We
also send him packages with food. But, you understand, "the more
the better." Poor guy he has already been away from home for 12
months.
Only today we have had the first warmer day. Until now there have
been heavy freezes.
Salo still works at Gold's; although his boss is gone. He's an
administrator.
The people who have 'kept' him consider him 'indispensible'. You
know how hard working and 'courageous' he is.
We are living with my brother- in-law, Maks and Abraham Zub.
I would very much like to be with our parents already, but at this
moment it is very difficult to move.
How far is La Panne from Brussels? Is Kazik in Paris?
I am constantly worried about you. How does the baby feel in a
strange environment? Does she sleep well?

The Goldberg's are in Warsaw; at least Monia, Lila, Romka and
Mietka are in Warsaw. The rest are in Lodz. They all live together.
After 5:00 pm we meet with friends. Besides that, I wait for letters
from you, Lolka and Mom and Dad.
So, write because that is our only joy.
We squeeze and kiss you,

Renia, Salo and Marcys

No. 2 April 29, 1940 Last night of Passover
Otwock, Poland to La Panne, Belgium

Dearest Halu,
Today we received your post card which answers my card. Now
perhaps you will stop complaining that we don't write very much,
because we answer every card and even write in between. I am
repeating once again that you should not send any packages – don't
even think about it at all. As you know from March, 1939, I was in
the neighborhood of Poznan. After that on the 1st of September, you
probably know what happened. There was a crazy heat (furious
activity). It was very hot. But on the 19th of September, it finally
ended and after a couple of weeks "they" sent me to Oleska from
where I returned home just for the holiday. Why this happened,
I'll tell you when we have the chance. Alas, I am not able to write
everything that happened to me during this year in one letter, but I
will try to write a little something in every letter that I write. Please
write to us about our friends as fast and as much as you can. Give my
best regards to Ignas, and Yvonka,   See you. Lolek

Dearest Halu,
Here it is the last night of Pesach (Passover). We spent the holiday rather pleasantly. Even Maks was here for the entire two weeks for a rest. Recently I went to Warsaw, but I didn't see any of our friends. Maks is getting along pretty well in Warsaw. He even brought me very pretty sandals. Here they are very fashionable and comfortable. Sweet regards for Ignas, Yvonka.   Fredza

My family always leaves me so little space that I can never write to you. So, I am sending only regards and kisses,
                                        Lily

Dearest Halinko,
I thank you very much for remembering Marcys's birthday. I couldn't tear your present out of his hands.
                              Renia and Marcys

Regards and kisses for Yvonka, Ignas and yourself,
                                        Maks

No. 3 Winter 1940-41
Warsaw Ghetto to Figueira da Foz, Portugal

Dearest Hala,
We are very grateful for your concern for us and our welfare. For the moment we feel good and do not want for anything. From now on please stop trying to send us packages, because they are not necessary. What we need is news of our friends. In a previous letter I asked about Anki Pinchevski.

Dear Halu,
I don't know how I am supposed to understand it. Is it possible that we will live together? The joy is so great that I think of only this. How will it be? What Ignas thinks of this? Because he wasn't for it. We brought linens and things with us when we left. We have a

beautiful day today and everybody is out for a walk. Why doesn't Ignas write? I am finishing and I send you and Yvonka best regards.
                              Kisses, Mother

My Dear Girls,
At this moment, we just came back from a walk. We had a nice meal – eggs and onions. Our Passover Seder was very nice and Marcys asked the four questions. Grandpa was delighted. Grandma is also satisfied. Salo is still in Lodz. Fredza and Maks are in Warsaw and they will come here tomorrow.

                    I kiss you strongly, Renia and Marcys

No. 4 Winter 1940-41
Warsaw Ghetto to Figueira da Foz, Portugal

Dear Halu and Ignashu,
We just got your card that informs us that you have intentions to go to the USA. Imagine that Maks's sister Mila also went to New York. Or, she may still be in Lisbon, but we write to her in the USA.
Hank Biatogotowska is also in Lisbon.
We now live in Warsaw. Our parents on Zelazna and I on Nowolipka very close to Mali Spiro.
I am already longing to see Yvonke. I adore children of her age. Lately I am earning a little money by knitting. Maks is very courageous.
Henio Bankier got married to Zotorrejczkowna, they are in Warsaw. I can't write everything because they wouldn't be any space left for others.
Maybe one day we will still have a long chat. I am in a hurry now because I have to help with lunch.
                                        Fredza

Write to: Puchalski, Stefan
Ul. Wolska n. 50/29
Kindest regards, we hope to see you as soon as
possible.

> *Heniek, Yulia, Miriam*

Best regards and see you soon.

> *Salo*

Dearest Halu and Ignashu,
Don't wonder why we haven't written in such a long time because it is
was very difficult to send post from Otwock. Now that we are here in
Warsaw letters will be easier to send.

> *From Lolek*

No. 5 Winter 1940-1941
Warsaw Ghetto to Figueira da Foz, Portugal

Dearest Halinku,
Maks wants to go to the USA. Maks has the most direct intention to
go there where you are but here nothing is sure.
Lately Maks was sick he had stomach problems, but thanks to a strict
diet he is better.
You can't imagine how we would like to see you. In the meantime, I'll
finish.

> *I kiss you all, Fredza*

*

I send you fondest regards and kisses, Dawid

*

I am sending you kindest regards and address Anki, sister of this
friend Shaw Allenby 23, dom Klajmana.

> *Lolek*

My Dearest,
We are waiting patiently for a letter from you and my sister together in
New York. We have the greatest hope to see you there.

> *Maks*

My Dears,
I am already studying with Mr. Sigmund Gross. He is our cousin. All
our family loves Yvonka. I wish you the best,

> *Marcys*

My Dearest Halinko,
As you can see my son is already literate. He does exams, reads and
writes fluently in Polish and Hebrew.
He has a nice height but is thin, most importantly he is healthy.
You can't imagine how he loves his grandma. He tells everyone that no
one on earth has a grandmother like he does – except Yvonke. From
that milk that you sent, he didn't want to drink not even one drop
without sharing it with his grandma. When will Yvonke have the
same experience?
Any time now, Salo is going to get some work outside of Warsaw. He
can't wait because until now he hasn't been earning. How is Ignas
getting along? Does he have some possibilities for earning something?
Is your departure already determined?
I squeeze you all tightly,

> *Renia*

Dearest,
I send you my fondest regards. In the next few days I will be going
out of Warsaw as a director of a camp with a salary of 300 zloty

monthly. I am very happy about this.
Write often and detailed. What is Ignas doing?

Regards, Salo

My Dearest,
As usual Renia has written so much that I have to rack my brain to
think of something to write.
So, I will tell you that I miss you very much. I hope to see as soon as
possible. Here we all feel fine and are healthy.
And, to tell you what is going on here we would need days and nights.
There is only the fear that we will not be able to remember everything.
You wouldn't believe what a snake Yula is! Only after so many years
have I gotten to know her after so many years. It's a pity for every
regards you send to her. You are surprised, aren't you? But we don't
give ourselves.
Hala. Don't send chocolates and marmalade. We don't need luxuries. I
kiss you long and strong.

Mother

Best regards to Mme. Krakowiak.

No. 6 July 10, 1941
Warsaw Ghetto to Figueira da Foz, Portugal

My Dears,
After almost three months, when we had practically resigned from
ever getting the 5 kilo package, from out of the blue, on July 8ᵗʰ there
finally came the notice to show up for a package from Portugal.
In the beginning there was a fight. Who would go? And then when
destiny fell on Lily and Lolek, there started to be misgivings about
whether the package was actually .5 kilos instead of 5 kilos. And, so
on…
It is really hard to describe the scene in words. So, finally, when the
night had passed and the day was breaking Lolek and Lilka stole
from the house and after a couple of hours they triumphantly brought

home all the magnificent things and with great reverence and the
assistance of the whole family were unpacked.
Summer in the city is quite sad. Here, the color green is a rarity.
However, we do not lose hope to see you again some time.
I kiss you strongly,

Renia

My Dearest,
We finally received that long desired package that everybody drooled
over for which we thank you very much.
But, there was no sign of a letter from you. Why do you write so
rarely? In the end I explain it to myself by saying that you are
preoccupied with your departure. I would really like you to meet Maks
sister. You probably received a letter about her already.
Now we are very worried about Lutek Gross. Here there is nothing
new. We are living somehow. The summer is easier, but winter will be
here soon.
Kiss Yvonku and send us her picture. They are for us the most
beautiful film.

Freda

My Dearest,
We received the wonderful package for which we that you kindly. We
had a lot of joy and satisfaction. The whole family assisted in the
unpacking. I triumphed.
And now what is good with you.
When are you leaving? How is adorable Yvonka? Does she feel well?
Has she changed?
We are all well? I am sending you my fondest regards,
I kiss you and squeeze you.

Mother

My Dearest.
According to your wishes I am detailing what we received:
Soap, flour, noodles, rice, coffee, cacao, tea, two tins of sardines, meat,

chocolate, sugar.

Since grandpa can't get tobacco here, it would be nice if you could send some packages.

Write every week.

Lolek

No. 7 September 23, 1941
Warsaw Ghetto to Figueira da Foz, Portugal

My Dears,
We received the sardines and the chocolate which we ate on the spot. We changed the sardines for meat. We thank you kindly for everything.
A few days ago, I got a letter from Fredza that she received the cocoa and money. Life is cheaper there than here. She is very glad to be there.
Here everything is the same. We are all, for the moment, thank G-d, healthy.

Renia

Dearest Hala,
If you can, send us some wool for sweaters in a brown color. If you can't afford it, so stop sending packages altogether. Because in the meantime things have gotten a little better for us, since Lolek is working and Salo is also working.
I squeeze you strongly,

Mother

Dearest Halu and Ignashu,
On the occasion of the New Year I am writing to you. I am learning well and in one month I am finishing the 3rd grade.
Kindest regards and kisses,

Marcys

No. 8 September 30, 1941
Warsaw Ghetto to Figueira da Foz, Portugal

My Dearest,
On the occasion of the New Year I am sending you the kindest greetings for a Happy New Year. I received coffee and Fredza also received coffee and cinnamon for which we thank you kindly. In further packages, Fredza asks for cocoa without sugar.
News from you lifts our spirits, although I have stopped believing that something will change some day.
What's new with you? How is sweet Yvonka getting along?
Here thank G-d everything is good. We will probably have to change apartments.
I am ending because I have to leave space for others.
Kisses and Best regards,

Mother

Dear Halu,
With regards to our changing our address: I. Gross, Nowolipie 10/49. Try to send only cinnamon, cacao without sugar, and finally brown coffee not too roasted and not too little roasted.
Kindest regards and best wishes,

Lolek

81

No. 9 October 9, 1941
Warsaw Ghetto to Figueira da Foz, Portugal

My Dearest Halu,
We recently received ½ kilo cacao, ½ kilo coffee, ½ cacao with vanilla.
The cinnamon really paid off. We "pull out" 2.50 zlote for one deca
gram. I don't permit the cacao to be sold because that "cereal" coffee,
especially without milk, doesn't belong to the best type of beverage.
Mama, Papa and Marcys absolutely must have something nutritious,
because their weight leaves much to be desired.
Lilka and I are holding ourselves surprisingly well.
Fredza went to the provinces and they are now eating their fill. She
will probably feel better in a very short time.
Salo is in Sandomiez. Lola Greb, her husband and child went to
Włodzimierz. She writes that she is very please, because she had it
very bad here.
We are terribly worried about Alka. She is very bad, but I have spoken
to people here who understand her sickness very well and they say you
can live with it for a year or even two. Only you could kick the bucket
faster from the surroundings than the sickness. Whichever comes first.
My dear, Write often about how he is doing, you know how close we
are with them.
And, how very interested we are in his fate.
We could have so easily been with Anka Pinczewska if not for our old
"cheapskate" (Abram Majer), we could have gotten away many a time.
When are you going to see Mr. Forman? Is that still a possibility?
Because, I already have stopped believing in it.
When you see Yusek Groner give him regards from Melie Szocter, She
is here in Warsaw and is managing well.
Marcys is very capable. He reads and writes beautifully in Polish as
well as Hebrew.
Now he will be going to the 4th squad (grade). And he is very capable
and independent;
Lolek's willing "adiutant" (lower ranking officer, assistant). He also

helps Grandma in taking care of certain business. He always
"knows" everything first.
How is your little lady? Tell Ignas to write?
I kiss you all, strongly regards,

> *Renia*

My Dearest,
I kindly thank you for the package. You already know everything.
My family has gotten a little smaller and because of this I am
relieved.
Fredza received the cacao. I see Mrs. Obtrembne very often. She
looks very bad. Gray as a golem (a mystical creature created from
dust). She makes a bad impression. I am also a little thinner, but I
am not grey yet.
What is good by you? How does sweet "papcia" feel?
Renia is sitting next to me and is forcing me to write that Marcys
is a genius.
I am sending you sweet regards and kisses,

> *Mother*

(Renia again)
I would prefer to be sitting next to you so that you could see this
with your own eyes.
Maybe you have any old or unneeded suit, sweater or men's shirt?
Because Marcys has out grown or worn out everything. It would
be very helpful. R

Dear Halu and Ignashu,
I won't add anything new because I have already been "overtaken".
Best regards,

> *Lolek*

Glossary

Bathinette
baby bath and changing table combination.

BBC
British Broad Casting radio station.

Blitzkrieg
a method of warfare, with a concentration of armored and motorized or mechanized infantry.

Canasta
a card game popular in the 1950s.

Cherub
a winged angelic being.

General Gouvernament
(General Government) a self-governing territory under the Nazis occupation. Poland was divided into three self-governing territories.

Ghetto
an enclosed part of a city, occupied by a particular group of people, in this case forced enclosure of Jewish people by Nazis.

Hala
nick names: Halina, Halinka, Halu, Halinko, Halinkon.

Ignas
(ig-NASH') nick names: Ignatius, Ignashu, Ignasiu.

Jiu-Jitsu
a Japanese martial art.

Jerry can
a container for fuel (gasoline) for a car.

Kibbutz
a collective community in Israel traditionally based on farming.

Lolek
nicknames: Leon, Lejb (Jewish name).

Maccabi Warsaw
a multi-section Jewish sports club established in 1909.

Maginot Line
a line of concrete fortifications, obstacles and weapon installations that France constructed on the French side of its borders with Switzerland, Germany and Luxemburg during the 1930s.

Mandate Palestine
the League of Nations called upon Great Britain to facilitate the establishment of a Jewish national home in the Land of Israel, July 1922.

Nazi Party
the National Socialist German Workers' Party lead by Adolph Hitler, 1921-1945.

Nuremburg Laws
the laws issued in 1935 by the German government to further the legal exclusion of the Jews from German life.

Partisan
a member of an organized body of fighters who attack or harass an enemy, especially within occupied territory; a guerrilla.

Purim
a Jewish holiday where people celebrate by wearing costumes.

Sesta
a midday rest typical of warm countries.

Yom Kippur
the most solemn religious fast day of the Jewish year.

Wansee Conference
assembly of the powers of the Nazi Party; term "Final Solution" designated there, January 1942.

Zionism
(Zionist, adj.) a political and cultural movement calling for the return of Jews to build a Jewish State in the Land of Israel (Mandate Palestine).

Permissions and Credits

All of the photographs and documents in this book come from the private collection of Joan Arnay Halperin, except for those noted below:

P. 7 Posiedzenie Komitetu Nadzczego (Lodz City Council), circa 1925. Image courtesy of the City of Lodz, Poland.

P. 20 Restored Nazi road signs. Image courtesy of the Local History Archives Alois Schwarzmüller, Garmisch-Partenkirchen, Deutschland. Exhibition November 2006. The Winter Olympics in Garmisch-Partenkirchen 1936 "The Spirit of the New Germany".

P. 31 Map of Europe. Design by Fiona Cashell. Image courtesy of the Sousa Mendes Foundation.

P. 34, 39, 41, 42, 43, 73 and 74. Images courtesy of the Sousa Mendes Foundation.

P. 35 L'Exode, France, 1940. Image courtesy of Wikimedia Commons. Source: Bundesarchiv, Bild 146-1971-083-01 / Tritschler / CC-BY-SA 3.0.

P. 36 Heinkel He 111, a German bomber. Image courtesy of Wikimedia Commons. Source: Royal Air Force Battle of Britain campaign diaries.

P. 44 Hitler's army marching through Paris, June 14, 1940. Image source: Allgemeiner Deutscher Nachrichtendienst - Zentralbild (Bild 183). Photographer: Folkerts.

P. 65-66 Bear Mountain State Park Swimming Pool. Copyright © Thoreau Lovell

P. 67-68 Whitestone Bridge. Attribution: Image courtesy of Dav5nyc at the English language Wikipedia.

Back Cover Bio Image: Fiona N. Cashell

In addition, we wish to thank all of the institutions and individuals who graciously gave their permission to use photographs/documents in this book. The individual photo captions include the names of these institutions and individuals. We apologize in advance for any unintentional error or omission. If it should be brought to our attention, we will make all reasonable efforts to rectify the error or omission in subsequent editions.

Resources

KAPLAN FAMILY
"Jewish Members of Lodz City Council, 1919-1939."
Welcome to Jewish Lodz. Accessed February 20, 2017. http://
kehilalinks.jewishgen.org/Lodz/noted.htm#Community
Leaders.

KRAKOWIAK FAMILY
"Makbi." Virtual Shtetl. Accessed February 20, 2017. http://
www.sztetl.org.pl/en/term/446,maccabi-in-poland/
"Ha Shomer Hatzair." Jewish Virtual Library. Accessed
February 20, 2017. http://www.jewishvirtuallibrary.org/
hashomer-hatzair.
"85 years, one kibbutz." Ynet News. Accessed February 20,
2017. http://www.ynetnews.com/articles/0%2C7340%2CL-
3360367%2C00.html.

PRE-WORLD WAR II
"Nazi Laws on Jews Put into Effect." Jewish Telegraphic
Agency (JTA). Accessed February 20, 2017. http://www.jta.
org/1935/09/17/archive/nazi-laws-on-jews-put-into-effect.
"Berlin, Preparing for Olympics, Removes Last Anti-Jewish
Signs." Jewish Telegraphic Agency. Accessed February 20,
2017. http://www.jta.org/1936/04/09/archive/berlin-preparing-
for-olympics-removes-last-anti-jewish-signs.
"40 Private Refugee Bodies Form United Front at Evian."
Jewish Telegraphic Agency. Accessed March 12, 2017. http://
www.jta.org/1938/07/08/archive/40-private-refugee-bodies-
form-united-front-at-evian.

WORLD WAR II
"Battle of Bzura River." Youtube. Accessed February 20, 2017.
https://www.youtube.com/watch?v=ZKejEKt70FA.
Engelking, Barbara, and Jacek Leociak; translated by Emma
Harris. *The Warsaw Ghetto: A guide to the perished city.* New
Haven: Yale University Press, 2009. Print.
"Jewish Congress Urges World Action Against Treatment
of Jews in Poland." Jewish Telegraphic Agency. Accessed
February 20, 2017. http://www.jta.org/1939/12/07/archive/
jewish-congress-urges-world-action-against-treatmen-of-jews-
in-poland.

BORDEAUX, FRANCE
Sousa Mendes Foundation. Accessed February 20, 2017.
http://sousamendesfoundation.org/
"Bordeaux Crowded with Refugees; Jewish Groups Plan
Emergency Offices." Jewish Telegraphic Agency. Accessed
February 20, 2017. http://www.jta.org/1940/06/05/archive/
bordeaux-crowded-with-refugees-jewish-groups-plan-
emergency- http://www.historynet.com/lisbon-harbor-of-
hope-and-intrigue.htm offices.
"Barbed Wire Thrown Around Warsaw Ghetto." Jewish
Telegraphic Agency. Accessed February 20, 2017. http://www.
jta.org/1939/11/21/archive/barbed-wire-thrown-around-
warsaw-ghetto#ixzz2qxxOrHxe.

PORTUGAL

"Jews Press Efforts to Escape from France; 760 More Reach Portugal." Jewish Telegraphic Agency. Accessed February 20, 2017. http://www.jta.org/1940/07/14/archive/jews-press-efforts-to-escape-from-france-760-more-reach-portugal.

American Jewish Joint Distribution Committee (JDC). Accessed February 20, 2017. http://www.jdc.org/.

"Portugal Fears Loss of Freedom if Nazis Drive for Gibraltar; Gestapo Lists Jews." Jewish Telegraphic Agency. Accessed February 20, 2017. http://www.jta.org/1940/07/15/archive/portugal-fears-loss-of-freedom-if-nazis-drive-for-gibraltar-gestapo-lists-jews.

"Nazis Let Jews Leave Poland on Payment of $750." Jewish Telegraphic Agency. Accessed February 20, 2017. http://www.jta.org/1941/01/17/archive/nazis-let-jews-leave-poland-on-payment-of-750-emigration-from-lithuania-spurred.

"Britain Will Allow Stranded Polish Jews to Enter Jamaica." Jewish Telegraphic Agency. Accessed February 20, 2017. http://www.jta.org/1942/01/09/archive/britain-will-allow-stranded-polish-jews-to-enter-jamaica.

"JDC Arranges Emigration of Polish-Jewish Refugees from Lisbon to Jamaica." Jewish Telegraphic Agency. Accessed February 20, 2017. http://www.jta.org/1942/01/12/archive/jdc-arranges-emigration-of-polish-jewish-refugees-from-lisbon-to-jamaica.

GIBRALTAR CAMP, JAMAICA, BWI

Cooper-Clark, Diana. *Dreams of Re-Creation in Jamaica: The Holocaust, Internment, Jewish Refugees in Gibraltar Camp, Jamaican Jews and Sephardim.* Victoria: FriesenPress, Inc., 2017. Print.

"Polish-Jewish Refugees in Jamaica Seek Permanent Haven Elsewhere" Jewish Telegraphic Agency. Accessed February 20, 2017. http://www.jta.org/1942/04/07/archive/polish-jewish-refugees-in-jamaica-seek-permanent-haven-elsewhere.

The Center for Jewish History. YIVO Institute. HICEM Archives. Accessed February 20, 2017. http://www.cjh.org/, https://www.yivo.org/.

SKELETONS

"Passengers sailed SS Serpa Pinto, destination Jamaica: January 24th, 1942 (id: 31562)." Accessed February 20, 2017. https://resources.ushmm.org/vlpnamelistimages/ReferenceCollection/AC0366/AC0366.PDF.

"Children During The Holocaust." United States Holocaust Memorial Museum. Accessed February 20, 2017. https://www.ushmm.org/wlc/en/article.php?ModuleId=10005142.